YUKON RIVERBOAT DAYS

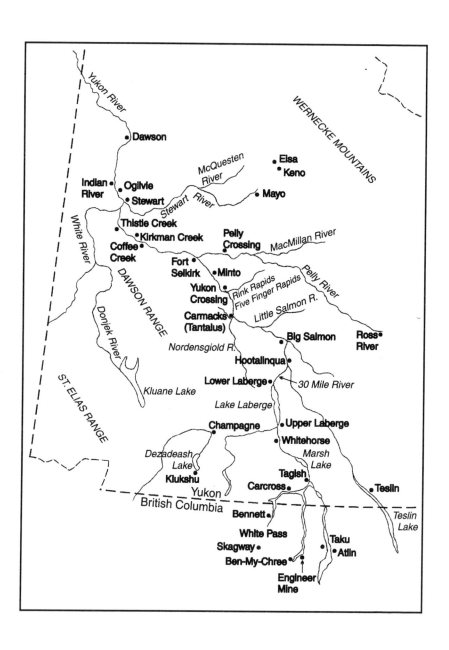

YUKON RIVERBOAT DAYS

Joyce Yardley

hancock house

ISBN 0-88839-386-5

Cataloging in Publication Data
Yardley, Joyce, 1925-
Yukon riverboat days
ISBN 0-88839-386-5

1. Yukon Territory—Biography. 2. Steamboats—Yukon Territory—History. 3. Frontier and pioneer life—Yukon Territory. I. Title.
FC4022.1.A1Y37 1996   971.9'102'0922   C96-910028-0
F1095.Y9Y37 1996

Production: Myron Shutty
Editing: Nancy Miller
Front Cover Photo: The sternwheeler *Yukon* pushing a barge. *Yukon Archives: C. Tidd collection*
Back Cover Photo: Joyce Yardley. *J. Neil Newton photo.*

Photo credit abbreviation key:
UAA: University of Alaska Archives
MM: MacBride Museum
AH: Atlin Historical Society
UW: University of Washington
MLB: Martha Louise Black

Published simultaneously in Canada and the United States by

HANCOCK HOUSE PUBLISHERS LTD.
19313 Zero Avenue, Surrey, B.C. V4P 1M7
(604) 538-1114   Fax (604) 538-2262

HANCOCK HOUSE PUBLISHERS
1431 Harrison Avenue, Blaine, WA 98230-5005
(604) 538-1114   Fax (604) 538-2262

Contents

————◆—◆—————

This book is dedicated to the memory of the brave and hardy pioneers, who lived and worked and raised their families along the Yukon River in the days of the paddlewheelers.

Introduction

Many books have been written about the Klondike gold rush of 1898, and the paddlewheelers that plied the waters of the mighty Yukon and its tributaries. Much less attention has been paid to the folks who lived along the shores of the river; between the main centers of Dawson City and Whitehorse, in the Yukon Territory.

There were times, when I was writing this book, that I found myself in a kind of 'time warp.' The period of my life as a child, growing up in Whitehorse in the decade between 1930 and 1940, became the present, and I was looking back from there to the turn of the century. The early years on the Yukon River, about which I was writing, seemed much closer from that perspective and I found it easier to identify with the folks whose stories I have told here (many of whom I knew personally as a child, as 'older people'). Some of these folks have since passed on, but have left this account of their personal experiences. Others are very much alive, having come to the Yukon in the more recent days of the riverboats.

Many of these true-life chronicles are excerpts from personal interviews with Yukon old-timers, taped in the mid-1970s. In fact, one gentleman, Mr. Frank Goulter, was 102 years old at the time with a memory that would put a lot of much younger people to shame.

I am proud to have this opportunity of passing these fascinating memoirs on to you. They should not be allowed to die, unheard. Together, they form a colorful mosaic of the early history of the riverboat days in the Yukon. Included here are woodcutters, riverboat men, mounties, and trading post operators, and the wives and families of these men.

I have gathered information from the following sources: personal experiences and memories; stories related to me by relatives of some of the people mentioned here; and various interviews collected on tape by Cal Waddington, without whose cooperation much of this book may never have been written.

Thanks also go to Phyllis Simpson, the eldest daughter of Happy and Pauline LePage; Betty Taylor, the late Charlie Taylor's wife; Mr. G. I. Cameron; and Heather Jones from the Yukon Archives.

I

Life on the Yukon River

1

The LePage Family

—◆—

Oh, dear little cabin, I've loved you so long,
And now I must bid you good-bye!
I've filled you with laughter, I've thrilled you with song,
And sometimes I've wished I could cry.
Your walls they have witnessed a weariful fight,
And rung to a won Waterloo;
But oh, in my triumph I'm dreary tonight—
Good-bye, little cabin, to you!

Robert Service

Happy LePage lifted Pauline into his arms and carried his wife
across the threshold of the cabin.

"Welcome to your new home," he said proudly. All she
could do was stare. She walked over to the wall, leaned against
it and just looked. She didn't know whether to cry or laugh.
Her husband got the fire going, made some scrambled
eggs...and she was home.

"My first home. God, when I think of it now..." she said. "I
was raised in a family of three boys and a sister. I had so many
kids to play with. Then, when I went to work, I always had a lot
of friends to hang around with. And then to go to a place like
that, I thought I'd dropped from heaven to hell. I had never
been so lonely in my whole life as I was then."

Happy LePage came to the Yukon in 1926, and worked on

the SS *Casca,* which was one of the steam-driven paddlewheelers that carried passengers and supplies up and down the Yukon River. He had the job for two seasonsand then decided he could make better money cutting wood for the boats. The next fall he went to Three Rivers, Alberta, where he met and married Pauline in 1928.

Pauline was born in Germany in 1907 to an Austrian mother and father. Happy brought her back to the Yukon, where they went directly to Rink Rapids, a spot along the river miles from any civilization where Happy had his wood camp. He had been all alone there, until now, staying in the small log cabin that he had bought, along with the wood camp, a horse and a wagon. For all this he paid $500, a fair price in those days.

The cabin was across the river from his camp, which was located on a good-sized island. It was just upstream and around a curve from the old SS *Dawson,* which had sunk there earlier and had been abandoned. Part of the boat was still on the bank along with a pile of rubble that was left there after the wreck. A person could step right from the bank onto the hull.

Happy had made a bed for himself out of poles, and he found a bed-spring on the rubble pile. Among the treasures on the heap, he had found a cache of tablecloths, which he utilized as a ceiling cover. In October, the last steamboat of the season had dropped off enough groceries for the whole winter. He had stored all the dried stuff; beans, rice, flour and so on, in a cache (a little cabin built up on stilts to keep the animals away). Meat was stored in another cache. The perishables were kept under the floor of the cabin, in a little cellar that had a trap door in the kitchen. This one was too small to go down into, you had to open the trap door, lean over and reach what you wanted while on your hands and knees.

Happy had made shelves from lumber he'd taken from the steamer *Dawson,* and the bone china dishes had also come from there. He used everything he could salvage off the boat, because he knew the White Pass steamboat company intended to blast it away, very soon.

When Happy and Pauline arrived in Whitehorse they stayed in the White Pass Hotel. The manager, Mrs. Viaux was wonderful, got out the ironing board, and did everything she could for them. But to Pauline it was another world—everything seemed so old-fashioned. She met Louis Moi's girlfriend, Audrey Harbottle, and two girls by the names of Annie Chambers and Margaret Jackson. Pauline remembers having dinner at Harold Wilson's. The next night, the Jack Elliotts had them over for the evening.

"Everyone in Whitehorse talked about steamboats and caribou," Pauline said, "that's all they seemed to be interested in. We had stopped in Carcross on our way from Skagway, and met Adele McMurphy there, she was a schoolteacher. And I met some of the steamboat people, who were going out for the season. They all talked about the boats and caribou, and I thought, 'My this is a strange country I'm coming to.' I wasn't interested in those things, because I knew nothing about them." That was all going to change in the years to come.

Pauline and Happy left Whitehorse on the 8th of November, with Louis Moi, who was going to help Happy cut wood, and two other passengers who were on their way to Mayo. They rode on the "stage coach" which happened to be a Model T Ford at that time. The drivers were "Spot Cash" Jim Breadon and Ernie Summerton. The passengers piled on top of the boxes of freight on the back of the truck, with a buffalo robe over and under them. Pauline was the only woman on the trip. The "stage" was the only public transportation going from Whitehorse to Dawson City, and points between, in the winter months. It took them two days to get from Whitehorse to Carmacks by stage. They left early in the morning, and got into Braeburn the first evening.

"That was a long day sitting on those boxes," Pauline said. "The roadhouse there was nice and warm, and that wood heat felt so good. The table was all set. Jimmy Robinson was running the place then. Boiled potatoes, canned peas, pork chops and pie, and we really thawed out. But then, when he showed us the bedroom...oh, boy, the sheets were cotton, and it was just like an icebox in there! You felt like you were sliding between two sheets of ice."

The next morning they started off for Carmacks. They didn't stay at the roadhouse there, instead they stayed with Tom Murray, the fellow who sold them the wood camp. Tom had a little fox ranch across the Nordenskiold River, on the outskirts of Carmacks. They stayed with him two nights, and then started off by boat the next morning down to the wood camp. Tom loaned them a little Yukon boat (made out of boards and sealed with pitch or sap from the trees, and unpainted). And he loaned Pauline his parka, which came almost to her ankles, because all she had until then was her knee-length navy coat and her slippers. She wasn't dressed for the cold, or the river.

"There was a little slush on the river already, I didn't know where on earth we were going. There was nothing...nothing...no buildings...we were floating on down and just above the Five Fingers we hit a bar, right in the middle of the river. And I got scared. I thought, 'Oh, I'm finished!' I didn't know anything about sand bars. Then Louis stepped out, and I thought, 'What the heck is he doing, getting out in the middle of the river like that,' He pushed the boat off the bar, and got back in. I thought, 'Gee, that's funny, what is he standing on?' Then he pushed us right off that mountain! I had never been in a small boat before."

After a while Happy made Pauline and Louis get out of the boat, and they climbed up a steep bank on the left-hand side of the river. There was just enough snow to make it incredibly slippery, but they made it to the top and walked along the edge of the bank, while Happy took the boat through the Five Finger Rapids himself. He didn't want to frighten Pauline any further, if he could help it. He picked up his passengers at the end of the canyon, and they continued their journey.

"We kept getting farther and farther back into the hills," said Pauline. "I didn't think we'd ever stop going back into those hills."

Finally they landed at their destination—Rink Rapids. Louis found a cabin close by to live in, and he and Happy took

13

off for the wood camp every morning. Both men were strong, very hardy bush men, the harder the work was, the better they liked it. Pauline was left alone, on the other side of the river, in the lonely little cabin. She was twenty-one years old. She'd get up on the table, where she could reach the window, and make a little spot in the thick frost that had built up on the inside of the glass by holding her hand against it until it melted. This way she could get a glimpse of the river and the bank out there, and then the hole would freeze right over again. She would do this for hours, hoping Happy would come home from work early that day.

As for Happy, he lived up to his name, and things had never been better, he thought. He had a nice warm cabin to come home to now, and a wife waiting there for him. Pauline never complained and he never guessed how miserable she really was.

As the winter wore on, she never got used to the solitude, and her loneliness only increased as day after dreary day passed by. Happy would get up before daybreak, rested, fresh and eager to get to work. "You don't need to get up, honey," he told his wife, "I'm used to getting my own breakfast, and you just sleep in. There's nothing for you to do." He didn't realize that she wanted something to do in the worst way. But she propped a pillow under her head each morning, and watched him flip the pancakes in the heavy, cast-iron fry pan. The cabin would smell of grease and smoke, and she hated it.

Just for fun, he'd always flip one over to her in bed, and she'd lie there eating the pancake—never taking her eyes off him. Too soon he'd blow out the lamp and be gone again for the day, and then she'd roll over and sleep some more. It got so that she slept later and later every day.

Pauline didn't have moccasins, and she didn't wear slacks. "Those days women didn't wear slacks like they do now," she said, "And I just wouldn't. I had a black pair of pumps, and a pair of two-tone slippers, with low heels, and that was all I had brought...and short dresses. We were wearing short dresses then."

That first winter they had mostly canned meat, until they

14

really started to crave some fresh beef, and ordered a quarter to be sent down from Whitehorse by stage. They had plenty of bacon and eggs, but the eggs would have to be frozen in the snow before too long, as they were getting pretty flavorful. There was a woodpile inside the cabin, which at first pleased Pauline when she saw it. Good, she thought, I won't have to go outside for it when the kitchen stove needs stoking. Happy had driven three-foot pegs into the wall, and the wood was stacked to the ceiling. The next day, though, it all had to go out, because Pauline didn't have any room to put her trunk. "The cabin was very small. There was a big heavy stove," she said, "then the bed, and then there was my trunk. That took up the one wall—that's how big the cabin was. At the head of the bed we had one chair, then the table, and in the corner was a washstand with a hole in the top for the basin to sit in, and a cupboard underneath for the slop pail. There was room on it for our little gramophone so we kept it there. We had thirty records and that's all. There was no radio. We got so tired of those thirty records, playing them over and over. Of course we had no cat and no dog. We had a little card table, I think that came off the *Dawson*, too.

"The little card table had black leather on top. The airtight heater came next and then the door to go outside. The other wall had a shelf for dishes and things, and there was a small window. Under that window Happy had made a small work table, with pegs driven in and boards on top. That was my work space. I had bought some pictures in the fifteen-cent store in Vancouver, I still have those, and I made bright floral curtains for the windows—sewed them by hand. We had heavy, dark green, battleship linoleum on the floor, over the hand-hewed logs. And that was our cabin."

The White Pass sent Bert Peterson and his gang down to blast some rocks out of Rink Rapids that winter, and they built a couple of cabins there for the men to stay in. Later on, Louis Moi went to do blasting work for Bert, and stayed in one of those cabins from then on. He celebrated his twenty-first birthday (in 1926) with Happy and Pauline, in their little home.

As the need for more help arose, Happy flagged some

Indians down, two families that were drifting down the river trapping muskrat, and put them to work. They set up their tents there by the wood camp. The LePages stayed at Rink Rapids until September, 1929. Then one day the word came that T. C. Richards wanted someone to take over the roadhouse at Yukon Crossing, as the White Pass would be needing it, and Pauline suddenly wanted that roadhouse more than anything in the world. She couldn't think of anything else. There would be people to talk to. She just had to have that roadhouse.

H. O. Laughlin had been the last one to operate it. Happy and Pauline had walked down to see him one time, in March. It was six miles down the trail, and she had walked in her short navy coat, and her little slippers. It was hard walking, her shoes kept slipping off the icy moccasin trail, and she was in her first pregnancy at the time. A blizzard came up along the way, but in the end they made it to the roadhouse. When they got there Pauline wanted a cup of tea in the worst way. "Oh, God," she thought, "I need a cup of tea right now, please." Finally he made them lunch, and after a short visit they left. At the time, they never dreamed they would be running that business someday.

That walk was the only "outing" Pauline had all that winter. Finally, though, when it got a little warmer, she started going across the river, to watch Happy and Louis cut. She saw the way her husband worked. One time he was splitting a stick that was all knotty and twisted. He had three wedges in it, pounding and pounding. She said, "Throw it away—why don't you just throw it away? Don't work like that, get another one instead." She thought he was just ruining his innards, she said. But Happy just laughed at her, and pounded all the harder until it split in half. "No stick's going to get the best of me," he told her. "That's the way he always worked," Pauline said. "If it had been me, I would have thrown that wood and said to heck with it, there's lots of other trees, eh? But that's just how he was, he was a hard worker and he loved it."

The long winter came to an end, finally, and Happy had to use a little boat someone had given him, to go to and from work on the island. He was working alone, and at lunch time he came out to the edge of the river and ate there because Pauline would be right across from him on the cabin side, where she could holler over to him. One day, she said, she was playing and splashing in the water, running up and down the river. "I'm coming over," she teased. It was a very hot day, and the water felt cool and lovely. All of a sudden she noticed a "swish-sh-sh" sound behind her. She turned around—and there was the SS *Klondike*, just rounding the bend, coming upstream on her maiden trip. This was the first time Pauline had seen one of the steamboats in the river. She ran to the cabin, got the camera, and took a picture of it. She was sure the captain must have seen her cavorting on the bank. "He must have thought, who in the world is that loony woman running around over there?" Pauline recalled, "but I was just teasing my husband."

That was the summer Pauline lost her first baby. It was stillborn. She had tripped and fallen on her back one day, and she thinks that was responsible for what happened. After that, she felt no more movements, but being totally inexperienced in these matters, she thought, "It'll be all right. I'm sure everything will be okay."

Later, Happy decided to go cruising for timber, although it was Sunday. Usually Sundays he would stay home, sharpen his saws and split wood for the cabin. This day, Pauline didn't feel like being alone, she was apprehensive about the fall and didn't feel well, but she never mentioned it to Happy. "Oh, I'll go with you," she said. It felt like a rope tightening and tightening around her waist, but it would go away, she thought. She just didn't want to stay alone. They got into the boat, and every time he pulled on the oars she thought, "Oh my God, it hurts, it hurts." They got over to the other side, and started walking over the rocks on the beach. She never once let on to Happy about the pains, and she didn't realize that they were labor contractions.

"I was a real greenhorn—you can be so darn stupid," said Pauline. "Walking up the beach, a pain would hit me and I'd sit down and rest. Never said a thing to Happy, and he'd sit

17

down with me and have a smoke. Didn't notice a thing. This kept on, I don't know how many times, and he'd do the same thing; he'd sit down and roll another cigarette." After awhile he came to a patch of trees he liked, and said he was going in there. Pauline said. "Do you mind if I just stay here?" Because she couldn't go any further. She wasn't going to walk through all that deep moss. So he went in and left her there. The pains were getting closer and closer, and she became very scared. Nothing there but the river flowing by, and the big tall trees behind her. She was all alone, and she thought, "Isn't he ever coming, why doesn't he come back right now?"

Finally he did come back, and they walked back down the beach, over the rocks, and got into the boat. The same thing happened, every time he pulled on the oars, it would hurt, and the pains came closer and closer. She just felt like throwing herself over into the water. They reached shore and Happy jumped out of the boat, and they went up to the cabin. Pauline went over and flopped on the bed. Happy sat at the table, and said, "I think I'll send Louis Moi a note and tell him about that stand of timber." Louis was in Whitehorse then, working on the boats.

Pauline must have groaned or something, because Happy looked at her suddenly and said, "What's wrong with you?" in a surprised voice. Then, at last, Pauline told him she was in labor. She knew now without any doubt. He came over to her, and said, "Are you sure?" But he didn't need an answer. This was it, the time had come. Pauline was lying on a blue and green, striped blanket, she remembers, and Happy flopped on his knees , covered up his face with his hands and cried.

Suddenly, there was a knock on the door, something they very seldom heard. A man had been drifting down the river, and he decided to stop in at the cabin. Anytime someone stopped in, which happened only in the summer, he would be invited for a meal. But this time Pauline was in labor, and Happy met him at the door and said, "My wife is very sick. She's going to have a baby, and we need a doctor badly. Would you call Whitehorse from Yukon Crossing, and get a doctor here on a plane as soon as possible?" and the fellow said, "Yes, certainly!" jumped in his boat immediately, and floated six miles down the river to the roadhouse.

"I don't know who that man was, and we never saw him again," said Pauline, "But I'd love to be able to just thank him for taking off like that without even a cup of coffee." Right after he left, she had one huge pain, and everything came out at once. Her husband picked the bundle up immediately and went outside, before Pauline could see it. She fell into a deep sleep, and when she woke up she realized what had happened. The pain on Happy's face told her that. She asked Happy if she could see it, but he told her no, it was better that she didn't. About four months had passed since her fall, and she had carried the baby all that time without any movement at all. Later, Mrs. Horsefall had told her that it probably had been dead during that time. "But I really don't know for sure," Pauline said, "I asked Happy what he had done, and he told me he had buried the baby. Baptized and buried it, he said."

Two days later Dr. Wride, arrived with T. C. Richards, who had brought him down the Dawson Trail. By then, of course, everything was over. "I was lying in bed, and the door was open," Pauline reminisced, "I could see the doctor coming, and he was walking behind T. C. Richards. He came in and asked a few questions, and examined me. He said everything was okay and they left soon after that."

Pauline wanted another baby right away, she said. But then they found out that Lochlin was going to leave the roadhouse at Yukon Crossing, and she pleaded with Happy to take it. He didn't take kindly to the idea at first, because he didn't want his wife working, but finally she persuaded him. If she had only had a sewing machine, or some paints, or anything, it would have been different, but she had nothing like that to keep her occupied.

Little by little, Happy moved their things over across the river with the boat, and left them on the shore. When the time came to move the horse and wagon, one of the steamboats took them across. Helping folks move their outfits from place to place was a common occurrence for the paddlewheelers. When Happy was leading the elderly horse up the steep bank, it stumbled and fell, and went somersaulting down the bank, where it wedged in between some trees. Happy had his ax with him, and he cut down one of the trees and got him out. Everything was fine then, until they came to a little creek close to the roadhouse, and they found the bridge was gone. A freak flood had taken it out in the spring, although it was dry now. They had to turn the horse loose, and carry the stuff over on foot.

Their first look at the building when they had arrived with their first load, told the rest of the story. Not only had the flood swept away the bridge, but it had also flooded the whole first floor of the roadhouse, leaving it in a terrible state, with silt piled around and over everything. They surveyed the damage with dismay, contemplating the hours and hours of work it was going to take to get things back in order. This was the spring of 1929, and the next flood happened in 1935, Pauline said, but they were out of there long before that. They stayed in the old telegraph office, a little cabin that Locklin had used when he first came into the country as a telegraph operator, and began the job of cleaning up the mess in the other building, using scoop shovels. There was an old caribou carcass, in a horrible state of decay, that had been left in the long wood-shed the winter before. The roadhouse had a wonderful big kitchen range that baked bread beautifully. They had never had such good bread. Just off the kitchen, in their bedroom, was a large airtight heater, and a big drum heater in the lobby. Made from oil drums, the heaters held three-foot logs which would last all night. But there was no heat in the spacious dining room, so by the time the dinner was brought in from the kitchen, it was cold before the guests were halfway through eating. Some of the passengers complained about it, Pauline said, so they had a heater put in there too. It took a lot of wood to keep the roadhouse heated. And they had to keep the barn heated too, because it was used to put the Caterpillar tractors in when they stopped over, otherwise they would never get going again in the morning.

Pauline was lonely no longer. She looked forward to the Cat trains, and really enjoyed the work and responsibility of running a lodge. Her job was to cook meals, wash dishes, make beds, do the laundry with a scrub-board, besides scrubbing the floors and keeping everything clean. They lived there and ran the roadhouse all that winter.

The next summer, Happy got another contract from White Pass to cut cord wood for the steamboats. Pauline went with him, back to the old camp at Rink Rapids, to their first cabin. By this time she was expecting another baby, and the ghosts of the past came back to haunt her when she was alone in the cabin. She began going with her husband in the boat, across the river to the wood camp every day. She abandoned her short dresses, and fancy shoes. Happy had made her buy some coveralls, which were far more comfortable for this life style. They had two extra wood cutters that summer, in fact Happy had employed them the previous fall, and they had been cutting there all winter.

Pauline packed lunches for Happy and herself, and stayed at the boat by herself, as it was quite a walk to where the men were cutting. But at least she was on the same side of the river. "Those were long days for me," Pauline remembers, "Just sitting there in the boat, waiting. Sometimes I'd get out and go up on the beach, walk up and down on the edge, but mostly I'd wait in the boat. Fighting off mosquitoes. Oh, those mosquitoes, they were so thick...they were just driving me crazy. I've never seen them so bad as they were that summer! I thought those days would never end."

Happy would ride over on the horse, and join her at lunch time, and they ate together in that little boat. Then he'd get back on the horse and go back into the bush again. One day Pauline decided to go for a walk on the beach, but the minute she put one leg over the edge of the boat, she felt a sharp twinge, and thought "Oh, oh, not again! I think it's too early for the baby. I'll just lie down in the boat and stay very still; maybe that will slow things down."

When Happy came back after work, he saw the boat, but no Pauline, and his heart stopped with fright. Coming closer, he saw her there, stretched out on the bottom. When her head came up, he started breathing again.

This time, when Pauline had discovered she was pregnant, she took no chances; she had planned ahead and got in touch with Mrs. Joe Horsefall, who lived at the village of Minto, and who had delivered many babies in her day. She was the local midwife in the area, and she had told Pauline that when her time was close, she would come and stay with her at the roadhouse at Yukon Crossing.

"What are you doing down there?" demanded Happy. "I think we'll have to take off," Pauline told him. With that, he just dropped the harness off the horse, jumped into the boat, and they were off. He had tried to talk Pauline into going to the hospital to have this baby, but she wouldn't hear of it. Dr. Ryde had sent them a bill for seventy-five dollars after she had lost the first one. "And for what?" she asked. His trip down cost them an extra hundred dollars. The LePages made one hundred dollars a month running the roadhouse. They had to work for almost two months to pay the bill. "Not this time!" she said.

The six-mile trip to the Crossing seemed to take an eternity, and he never stopped rowing, just as fast as he possibly could. Once there, he phoned Selkirk right away, because they knew the SS *Casca* was on its way upstream to Whitehorse. The operator said, "Yes, she's just coming around the bend now." Happy told him to ask the Captain to pick up Mrs. Horsefall at Minto, and bring her up right away.

"That was on a Monday," Pauline said. That evening Mrs. Horsefall took her on a long walk up the trail. "I thought, oh God, woman, can we please go back? But I never said anything, and finally she turned back to the roadhouse, and we all had a little snack, and went to bed." They had put an extra cot in their bedroom. About ten o'clock Pauline awakened them, and said she thought they'd better get up now.

They stoked up the fire and put some water on to heat. She could hear Happy pacing the floor in the kitchen. She knew he'd be chainsmoking, and she hollered to him. "Why don't you come in here?" The pains were getting pretty strong, and she needed some support. Just as he walked up to her, she doubled up with a huge contraction, grabbed Happy by his shirt at the chest, pulled him to her, and then threw him right back, where he fell into Mrs. Horsefall, knocking her against the table. It was an involuntary reaction to a piercing pain that came just then, and she seemed to have superhuman strength for a second. Pauline only weighed a little more than a hundred pounds normally...she was a tiny little thing...and they couldn't believe she had knocked them both off their feet at the same time!

In the next moment, she rolled over on her elbows and knees, and her little daughter Phyllis was born.

Pauline looked at her, she looked so white, even her hair was almost white. She thought, "Oh, thank God, she's so beautiful." Happy had made a bed for the baby some time before. He made it big enough to put a pillow in, and he had split some poles with an ax to make four legs for it.

An hour later, Pauline looked at the baby in that bed and thought. "One hour old. And you're living!" Then, "Two hours...you're two hours old!" And still later, "You're three days old, Phyllis. Oh please, don't leave us!" They named her Mary Phyllis Yvonne. She was born on July 1st, 1930, Dominion Day. She grew stronger and healthier every day, and gradually, Pauline got used to the idea that they weren't going to lose her.

The next time the steamer *Whitehorse* came floating by, it was decked with little flags, flying up one side of her and down the other. All for Phyllis...and life had never been so full and wonderful as it was then.

T. C. Richards wanted the LePages to run the roadhouse the following winter, but Pauline said, "No, the little girl comes first. I have something now, and I'm not sacrificing any of my time with her for some old roadhouse."

Mr. Locklin had given the LePages a little cabin that was just a few feet from the roadhouse, and now this was to be their home for a while. They built a kitchen onto it and Happy spread canvas over the wooden floor. Pauline painted everything blue and ivory, even the little card table they had brought from their first cabin at Rink Rapids. She sent out for some wallpaper she had seen in the Eatons catalogue. They had an old mattress that they draped a blanket over, and made into a couch by pulling half of it up the wall, and using the other half to sit on.

The LePages, and the new roadhouse operator, were the only people living at Yukon Crossing at that time. Their closest neighbours were Afe Brown and his family, down at Williams Creek, and the next stopping-off point was Carmacks.

In the spring of 1931, Louis Moi, who was on the mail service then, asked the LePages if it would be all right if his girl friend, Yvonne Besner, came from Whitehorse to stay with them for awhile, as he hadn't seen her in quite some time. Not long after she arrived, Bishop Stringer came through, by stage, on his way to Dawson. Louis and Yvonne decided to get married while he was there to perform the ceremony. They had the wedding right there in the LePage's cabin. "I had Phyllis all dressed in white," Pauline remembered, "and a fellow by the name of Stan Rickenson, one of the Cat drivers, gave the bride away."

Happy had a team of five dogs that year, and they bought a pet spaniel for Phyllis. It took a lot of caribou meat, Pauline said, to feed those dogs. Luckily there were hundreds of caribou, just streaming down from the hills on their migration, right across the river.

Those hills have since been named "Woodcutter's Range" by Dr. Smitheringale, a geologist, as a tribute to all the woodcutters who worked so hard to keep the steamboats running, for all those years. Pauline said there was also a range being named after the LePages (Mt. LePage).

Phyllis had no playmates at Yukon Crossing, just her little dog and her toys. She was good at entertaining herself, but when Phyllis was four years old, Pauline decided it wasn't fair for the little girl to be there with only adults for company.

So Happy moved his family to Whitehorse. He kept the wood camps, though, so in the winter months he was away from home a great deal of the time. He had crews doing most of the cutting, by now, at camps all along the river, and he hauled the wood out to the banks of the river. He also took on mail contracts. In the summertime, Pauline and Phyllis went back down river, and stayed with Happy, at whatever camp he was working at the time. In the summer of 1936, Pauline was expecting her second child. Happy was away at the wood camp at Rink Rapids, and he wanted the family to come and join him. Pauline went to see Dr. Duncan, to see if it would be okay if she went for a month. He advised against it, as she was seven-months pregnant. She walked out of the office, went down to the White Pass depot, and got a ticket to go on the SS *Klondike*. It's not as if I'm going in a small boat, she reasoned. As she was coming out of the depot, she ran into the captain of the SS *Whitehorse* and stopped to chat. When she told him her plans he said, "Oh, you don't want to go on the *Klondike*! Come on our boat, it's a much better one."

"No, the *Klondike*'s my boat." she teased. "I'm going on her." And the next morning she left, along with her little daughter, Phyllis, and Happy's cousin, Mary Adami, who was going down to join her husband, who was cutting wood for Happy.

As the big paddlewheeler pulled out from the wharf, Pauline began to have misgivings. Maybe I shouldn't be going on this boat, she thought. Why didn't I listen to the doctor, anyway? But it was too late, and they were moving into mid-stream, now. Standing there at the rail, looking down into the water, she reasoned with herself. Well, if anything should happen to this boat, the *Whitehorse* is right behind her anyway, so there's nothing to worry about. Nothing at all.

It was a beautiful morning; they had just got on the 30 Mile River, had enjoyed a lovely breakfast and were standing out on the deck talking, when the back end of the boat started spinning around, very quickly, and they could see she was going to hit the clay bank. When the boat hit, it lost control and started swinging, and when it swung, it hit a big rock that was jutting out into the river, and the side just caved in. The *Klondike* kept swinging and going downriver at the same time, sinking as she went along. The passengers stood there shocked, and helpless. The whistles started blowing an incredibly mournful sound that day, they seemed to bounce back and forth in those mountains, as if calling on the gods for help they knew would not be coming.

Pauline saw two young fellows with their bags, climbing off the boat, and she watched them in a daze, until she noticed that the deck was slanting at a crazy angle. Then she and Mary made a mad dash for the stateroom, taking Phyllis with them, but the door was jammed. Someone came along and pulled it open for them. Pauline grabbed a little case that belonged to Phyllis; it had some chocolate bars in it. Then she remembered that her big Pullman suitcase with Happy's good suit, her own embroidery that she'd been working on, and various other items, was already on deck. Of course, all that was lost. Pauline hopes that someone found it floating down river and made use of it. Happy's rifle, that she had been taking to him, was in the purser's office, where it was safe and eventually returned to the owner.

The women went back on deck and waited. Nobody seemed to get excited in spite of the fact that the boat was still sinking and drifting downstream. The boat was heading towards land now, and it seemed to Pauline as though the current was taking them at a terrific speed, and she had the feeling that they would hit shore with a bang. She took Phyllis and squatted down on the deck, waiting for the shock to come, but when the boat hit the shallow water, it just settled down gently. Then the lifeboats started coming down. The purser jumped off the boat with a typewriter in his arms, missed the boat by inches and hit the water. He was the only one on board who was hurt, Pauline said. He just banged his cheek up a bit.

Women and children first, they said. There were two young men in one of the lifeboats, and someone handed Phyllis over to them. Pauline looked into the boat and saw water coming into it in streams. She thought, "Oh, my god, we'll never make it in that boat, it's leaking too much." But she was the next one to get in, anyway. Then an older lady who needed a seat got on board, and took Phyllis on her lap. "I stood in the middle of the boat, with my feet planted apart to steady myself, and I could feel the cold water creeping up my legs. That's how fast the water was coming in. Poor little Phyllis held her feet up and kept saying, 'Mommy, we're going to drown! Mommy, we're going to drown!' I couldn't go to her, because I was afraid to move in case I upset the boat, and I stood still until the boat hit shore."

There was a nurse in the boat called Veronica Page, she was going into Mayo to work in the hospital there. Pauline said if it wasn't for her the boat would have sunk. She just kept bailing the water out like mad with a big pail. When they finally reached land, on a shallow sandbar, the nurse helped turn the boat over to empty all the water out. The two young men gave the survivors matches that they had somehow kept dry, and asked if they could manage by themselves for awhile. Veronica told them, "Yes, go ahead. We'll manage here just fine."

Pauline couldn't look back at the *Klondike*. She was so relieved to be on shore, because she she was certain they were all going to drown in that rowboat. "I knew we were goners." she said, "It felt just like the devil had his hand on my shoulder and was pushing me down into the water...that's the feeling I had. It was horrible. And I felt there's no use hollering or jumping or screaming...we've got to go down, and that's all there is to it. I heard afterwards that the men who were still on the *Klondike*, watching from the deck, were just shaking their heads, and saying, 'We'll never see them again.' I also heard that they let the horses and cattle that were on the boat go. I guess they swam to shore, but I never found out for sure."

So there they were, a group of women and a little girl, stranded on a sandbar. Besides Pauline, Phyllis, Mary Adami and Veronica, there was a tourist, Mrs. Dick Major, from Mayo, and Mrs. Cecil May, who was also going into Mayo. They wondered what had happened to the other lifeboats—none of them were in sight. Mrs. May was five-months pregnant and was lying down on the sand, crying, not knowing if she'd ever see her husband again. Pauline's suit was wet about three inches above the hemline. She took it off and threw it up on a tree to dry. Then it started to rain and it got soaked. The mosquitoes just about drove them insane. There were great clouds of them, ravenous for the taste of human blood. The only thing the women had to eat were the chocolate bars that Pauline had grabbed from her stateroom on the *Klondike*.

The accident had happened about eight o'clock in the morning, and the women were on the sandbar, until about three o'clock in the afternoon, when the fuel agent's boat (called a fuelage) arrived. They had brought oranges for them to eat.

The other passengers were scattered along both sides of the river, Pauline was told later, where the other lifeboats had dropped them off. Later that day they were all picked up by the SS *Whitehorse*, which very fortunately was on its way, a few hours behind the ill-fated *Klondike*.

The fuelage went over to the wreck, where they picked up blankets, food and some chairs, which they took back for the women on the beach. The men made tents from the blankets and treated the women like queens. They had all the good food they wanted and all the bananas they could eat, and life suddenly didn't look too bad at all. A float plane was sent from Whitehorse, piloted by Wasson, to check on their welfare. Soon it took off again, satisfied that everything possible was being done for the group. They waited there, thankful that they were alive, and enjoyed a campfire vigil, until the steamer *Whitehorse* came and picked them up about midnight.

Pauline got off at Carmacks, when they got there, and bought Phyllis a pair of coveralls, and herself a sweat-shirt, as they had lost all the clothes they had started out with. They continued on to Yukon Crossing, where Happy was waiting. Joe Gardiner walked them down the gangplank, Pauline said, and that was when she broke down for the first time. The next day she couldn't get her shoes on because her feet were swollen from standing in cold water for so long on the rowboat. She had to wear her husband's slippers for a day or two. Later, a parcel of clothes arrived from the Whitehorse chapter of the Imperial Order Daughters of the Empire. Everyone was so good, Pauline remembered.

For days after that, all manner of stuff floated down the river from the boat-wreck; the fishing was pretty good, at Yukon Crossing for a while. The LePages salvaged sacks of flour, that were still dry inside. The water had formed a crust on the surface, which sealed the inside and kept the flour in fine shape. They pulled an eiderdown sleeping bag out of the river, and it seemed that every day there were more goodies floating down from that boat. It kind of made up for the inconvenience of having Pauline's trip interrupted. "A lot of it probably made its way right to the Bering Sea," she said.

A couple of years after Amy was born, in 1938, the LePages bought a boat, called *The Ruby*. Pauline was getting tired of moving from cabin to cabin on the river. Each time she discovered the mice had moved in before them, and it was a continual battle to keep them cleaned out. So Happy bought the boat, which they converted into a houseboat. Their whole lifestyle changed right then, and it was wonderful, Pauline said. After the first trip down river, that was.

On that trip they were just coming into Lake Laberge, and Pauline was on the top bunk playing with the baby, when she noticed that the hose in place from the water tank to the pump in the kitchen had slipped out, and water was running onto the floor. In her hurry to jump down and put the hose back in place, she forgot to move the baby off the bunk in case she fell. When she was finished securing the hose in place, she suddenly remembered, and quickly turned back to the bunk. To her dismay, when she looked up, there was no baby in sight. Amy had disappeared. A stab of fear shot through her as she thought, "Oh, no! She's fallen off the bed and gone through that rotting canvas on the side of the boat!" (The canvas that Happy was planning to replace the next day.) But when she went out on deck there was Amy, safe in the arms of Phyllis. Apart from that, the trip was lovely. They brought the boat back upstream two more times, and then they just left it downriver, at one of the camps. The LePages were through with the cabins, and life was so much easier from then on.

"Kid" Marion, was the captain on one of the riverboats in those days, and he had a very creative sense of humor, which the tourists were treated to on every trip, whether they liked it or not. Pauline was the object of one of the jokes he liked to pull. Every time his paddlewheeler passed by the boat-house, that was anchored to the shore of the river..."You watch," he told his eager audience, "There's a crazy woman living on that boat-house. Every time we go by she runs and hides!" So they watched, fascinated, to see the crazy woman, and sure enough when they came close to the boat, there she was dragging her kids up the hill.

"Naturally," Pauline said, "I did take the two girls and go up on the bank, because when the boat went by it threw out such a wash that it would toss our little house around in the water, and I didn't like to be inside when that happened. So I got the reputation of being, 'That crazy woman.' That was me! I didn't hear that story until he had left the country—lucky for him, because I sure would have given him hell!" At other times "Kid" would tell his passengers to watch for the big, fat woman, who had to turn sideways to get out of a door. They would stand on deck, watching intently, and out of the houseboat would come this tiny woman, who still looked like a teenager. Fooled again.

Happy began looking for job opportunities in town after a while, in order to be closer to his family. After the war started, he worked on the construction of the Whitehorse, Aishihik, and Braeburn airports. "He was everywhere," said Pauline. He worked for John McIsaac, building the canal for the White-horse Dam, and was offered the job as inspector for the bridge at Carmacks. Even though a lot of their experiences were not happy ones, the LePages lived a very full life on the Yukon River over the years. "Except...at the time, I always felt that we were shut off from everything, too far away. If it was today, and we were living there," she said, "It would be different. There are roads everywhere now, and airports...you could jump on a plane and there you'd be. I'd do it all again, but it would be different. I would be interested in a lot more things next time around."

2

The Taylor and Drury Story

———•◆◆•◆•———

Some say God was tired when He made it,
Some say it's a fine land to shun.
Maybe; but there's some as would trade it
For no land on earth—and I'm one!

Robert Service

When I was a little girl, the town of Whitehorse, with its population of approximately 300, was the nucleus of my world. There was a vague awareness, somewhere in the depths of my mind, that *something* existed beyond the ends of town, because I heard the grownups talk of a place called Outside. But at the age of three, that concept was not in the range of my interests yet.

To me the most important part of town (apart from our home) was the place where my Dad went to work every morning. It was a store downtown, called Taylor and Drury. From the perspective of a small child, the building was enormous, and belonged to my Dad, (I thought) who very generously handed out to people anything they asked for.

Most folks in town in those days just signed for their purchases, and paid for them at the end of the month. Mom said they were charging things when they signed the papers. I could never figure out why Dad wouldn't give me everything I asked for in the store, too. When I asked my mother about this she'd say "We can't afford it." I didn't know that the stuff they called money had any purchasing value. It just didn't seem fair that those people could get anything they wanted from my Dad...*but not me!*

One day I stamped my foot in frustration and said, "Oh, can't afford it! Can't afford it! Why don't you just charge it?" My parents both looked at me in shock. I had never rebelled like this before. That evening I had my first lesson in matters of finance.

There were only two general stores in town, T & D (Taylor and Drury Co. Ltd.) and the NC (Northern Commercial Co. Ltd.). There was also a small corner grocery store run by John Sewell, close to the shipyards.

The story of Taylor and Drury is a fascinating one. The following is an outline of the history of the company, as told by Charlie, the eldest son of the Taylor family.

Charlie's father, Isaac Taylor, was from Yorkshire, England. He had been stricken with the dreaded tuberculosis, early in life, and had gone to the dry, sunny climate of Australia, to recover.

It was while he was there, hanging around the mines, that he heard about the gold rush in the Klondike area of the Yukon.

It took Isaac about a year to reach the Klondike the hard way; traveling the poor man's route into the country. He left Ashcroft with a group of men in 1898, one of whom was a fellow by the name of William Drury. They came up the telegraph trail to Telegraph Creek, B.C., and got locked in for the winter.

When spring came, Isaac made his way down the Stickine River to Wrangell; then on to Skagway, Alaska, where he found a job with the White Pass Co. working on the railway. When he heard about the gold being discovered in Atlin, B.C., he laid down his tools on the rails and set out for Atlin.

In the spring of 1899, he met up with William Drury, again, and the two men agreed to form a partnership. They had discovered, during the trials of the trip over the telegraph trail, that they enjoyed each other's company, and they felt sure they could get along well together in business. It was a good decision, because that was the start of a lifelong partnership, that neither ever regretted.

They realized that there was an opportunity in Atlin to make some money without having to mine for gold, and Drury said to Taylor, "I have a good outfit here, do you have any money?" Isaac replied that he had his last paycheck, (which was $200) and Will Drury said, "We're in business!"

So Mr. Taylor, who was a little shopkeeper from England, started buying old picks and shovels from men who had quit mining; either because they hadn't located any pay dirt on their property, or were just worn out trying. He took his purchases back to Mr. Drury, who had set up shop in a tent, and they sold them to the hardy individuals who intended to stay in the country. These men very quickly began to depend on Taylor and Drury, for their tools and outfits. It wasn't long before the firm was established. Soon they realized they were going to need another source of supplies for their business.

After a few months of operation, Mr. Taylor went out over the Fan-Tan Trail to Vancouver, where he bought up tons of supplies. On his return trip, he got as far as Lake Bennett, and there were hordes of people on the shore there, building boats and preparing for the last lap of their trip to Dawson City. He thought, "What's the use of lugging all this stuff to Atlin? We could sell it right here!"

He sent a telegram to his partner, saying, "Hey, the money is to be made right here, my man. Pull up your tent and come immediately. We'll set up here at Bennett." Mr Taylor had also bought a sewing machine, and plenty of canvas which the men needed for the boats. Drury was the man who could run a sewing machine, because he had been taught by his father back in Yorkshire.

So the first two Taylor and Drury stores started in B.C. Many of the sails seen in the archival photographs, of boats going down Bennett Lake on the first lap of the trip to the Klondike, were sewn by Will Drury. And many of the supplies carried in those boats were purchased from the company, as well.

By 1900, the railway to Whitehorse was completed, so the two men put their whole outfit on a flat car, and transferred it to Whitehorse. They started a small general store, close to the railroad, just south of the train station and facing Front St. They also opened a deluxe menswear store at another location on Front St., which was called The Bon Marche, and they operated both places for twelve years.

Then in 1912, 'Whitney and Pedlar,' who had a very influential business on the corner of Main and Front St. (1st Ave. now) became interested in the copper mining business. They founded the Kopper King mine, and they needed extra money for development. So between the two interests they formed the Taylor and Drury Pedlar Company, and the original two stores were amalgamated into one, and moved into the building on the corner lot, where it remained in operation for 75 years. That was the beginning of the dynasty, which soon spread all over the Yukon.

Everything went well with the Pedlar mining venture, at the Kopper King, until the end of the First World War, when the price of copper plummetted. "Off went their shirts, at that time," said Charlie, "and they had to get out, so they sold their share of the store business to my Dad and Mr. Drury. So from 1918 on, it went back to its original name of Taylor and Drury."

In 1901, the company started a branch store at Hootalinqua, at the confluence of the Yukon and Hootalinqua rivers. (The name Hootalinqua has now been replaced by Teslin, but for old times sake, I will refer to it by the original name.) For a time they carried on a brisk fur trade with the Indians there.

Another trading post was set up at the village of Carmacks, and soon Taylor and Drury went on to establish posts at the old fort of Selkirk, Ross River and Pelly Banks (where Campbell had an establishment in 1834). Over a period of some thirty years, they opened fifteen trading posts in the Yukon.

Many of the operators who looked after these stores were bachelors, and others married native girls and raised families in the Yukon. All the trading posts down river were really locked away from everyone in the winter months, because the fellows that ran them lived alone, and the Natives were all away trapping. At that time, Natives moved around like nomads, going back into the hills, and coming out periodically to sell their furs.

The storekeepers got $100 a month and found (found meaning room and board was supplied). They never had to keep track of what they used; when they needed a pound of butter, they just took it. Bedding and everything were supplied, and these fellows stayed in year after year.

"Some of them were worn out prospectors or disenchanted miners or trappers," Charlie told us, "but they were all very fine men. You could trust them with anything. Some of them had a very limited education, but they could bluff their way through. I used to watch the requisitions, and you'd see one come in that would have...two cases of cheese and one tom cat. And you'd know right away, that he was having trouble with mice. They would order traps, dog harnesses, candles, coal oil, lamps and matches. And in the food area, it would be coffee, tea, lard, flour, baking powder, sugar, salt, hardtack, bacon, beans, butter, raisins and dried fruit. And not much else; that was about all the staples.

"Roy Bottle was one of the storekeepers. When he retired he went out with around $30,000 that he had saved over his years of working for T & D."

Some of these men had relatively little or no education, but all of them, Charlie insists, were good and honest men. They would carry on, and remain at their jobs, sometimes for many years, and they had the toughness and stamina required for a job of that kind.

The branch stores, when they were established in the larger towns such as Mayo, Elsa and Carmacks for instance, required the storekeeper to have a higher education because there was all the accounting, book work and banking to be looked after. In these communities, there was a fair amount of competition, so the managers had to be merchandisers, as well.

In the fall of 1902, Will Taylor replaced George McCauley, who was due for a holiday, at the Little Salmon post. The steamers had stopped running for the season, and so Will was totally alone. All the Natives and trappers had gone into the hills. After a week or two had passed, Will later told the family he had started to have very strange sensations. He felt that in order to survive the isolation, and keep his self-discipline intact, he would have to establish a daily routine, and stick to it. So every day the ritual was the same. He would get up in the morning, wash and shave, and prepare himself a hearty breakfast. Then he went out into the store area, and checked everything over. Then he'd come back in, light up his pipe, and read a chapter of the Bible. (My most vivid memory of Mr. Drury was of that pipe. He was never without it.) Then he prepared his lunch, ate it, and went back into the store, where he swept and dusted everything, although there was not a customer around for miles. He did his laundry regularly, and kept his clothes immaculate.

Mr. Drury was a great reader, and that was his only entertainment in this place. He never let himself down, and kept this routine up every day for about two months; never seeing a soul in all that time.

Then, one day, just before Christmas, he heard the jingle of sleigh bells. He opened the door, ran out and hugged the first person that stepped out of that dog sleigh.

Will had left Mr. Taylor in Whitehorse to look after the store there, while he was away. "Ike," he said, "I won't be getting any mail here, it will all go to my mail box in town—so if you don't mind, I'd like you to open my mail and answer any correspondence that needs answering. I have brothers and sisters, and my mother is there, too. You might keep them up to date on what's happening. I'd really appreciate that."

So Ike told him he would look after it. In fact, he got a lot of pleasure out of getting to know Will's family, by mail. Especially his sister, Sarah, who was a schoolteacher in Lincolnshire. Before long, they had a lively correspondence going on between them. She had a very inquiring mind, and wanted to know all about the *aurora borealis*, the Arctic, husky dogs and many other things.

When the steamboats started running again, McCauley came back to his job, and Will went back to Whitehorse.

By this time Ike had decided it was time he had a trip back to the old country himself. He said, "Here's all your mail, Will. My mother passed away, and I want to go back and see her grave in Yorkshire. And I think I'll go and see your people, too, while I'm over there." Will replied, "By all means."

After Isaac had been gone for a few weeks, Will received a cable from him which said, "I married your sister, Sarah. Hold tough for a while longer. We're going on a honeymoon to Ireland." This turned out to be the big romance that went down in the history of the Taylor and Drury Company.

Sarah took to the Yukon right off the start. She found it intensely interesting, and wanted to learn everything about it at once, especially about the Natives. So Isaac, being very proud of his wife, took great delight in inviting Native women to go and have tea with her, when they came to town. Sarah would bake cookies, bring out her best bone china, and entertain them in style. There was only one custom of theirs that puzzled her, and she asked her husband about it later. "Ike," she said, "Why do these women, when they're through eating, take the rest of the cookies off the plate, and tuck them in their aprons to take home? It's such a strange thing to do." Isaac reminded her that if the cookies hadn't been so good, they wouldn't have done it! That was their way of complimenting her.

Taylor and Drury had been using a little gas-powered boat called the *Christine* up until 1905, which was not very effective for big loads. At this time they decided to build a steamboat. They called it the SS *Kluane*, and she was their pride and joy, a beautiful little paddlewheeler. It was good for twenty-five to forty tons of freight. She was built in 1905, on the T & D's own ways just above the White Pass shipyards. She traveled from Whitehorse, all along the side streams.

In 1915, Mrs. Sarah Taylor took the kids to Teslin Lake, where they had a family cabin, and they stayed there during the summer holidays, while their dad was running the store in Whitehorse. Charlie remembered how they used to enjoy those trips to the cabin. His mother loved that part of the world. She wrote a lot of her famous poems while they were there.

All the Taylor brothers had to take their turn at the branch stores. When the depression came, it was necessary for all the boys, Bill, Albert and Charlie Taylor, and their cousin, young Bill Drury, to roll up their sleeves and pitch in. The loss to the company during this time was terrific. Anyone who had an inventory item that was worth a dollar, found it had soon gone down to ten cents. In the meantime they had to pay the supplier the original dollar charged, then turn around and sell it for ten cents to the customer.

Taylor and Drury took a beating in the fur business, because it was a luxury item, and in a depression it is luxury that goes down the drain first. When the smoke all cleared, they had lost a quarter of a million dollars within two years because of the drop in fur prices.

"This really put our company to its knees," said Charlie, "and had it not been for the good credit rating of Taylor and Drury, we'd have gone down like so many Canadian companies, who were over-extended when the depression hit. But the suppliers said, 'If you go down, we go down,' and several of the large outfits in Vancouver saw us over the bad times, and we were able to get back on our feet again." It took the company ten years to get back to the strong trading position they had before the depression.

"Taylor and Drury went back to back with the Hudson Bay Company," Charlie said. "They had stores up in the Liard country, on the Yukon side, and we held quite an influence in there for years and years." The Selkirk store stayed in operation until after the end of the First World War.

In 1916, the Shushana and various gold strikes were going on in the Kluane area, and on the American side as well. The government wanted another transportation system, other than the *trail* to Kluane, which was very difficult to maintain, so they looked into the possibility of sending steamboats from the Yukon River, up the White River and its tributaries, all the way to Kluane Lake. The government even offered a $2500 bonus to any boat which would venture the trip as an experiment...providing they reached their destination...just to prove it could be done.

Taylor and Drury had a lot of orders from the Kluane area, so they took on the challenge of attempting to take their little steamboat *Kluane* up the White River to the village. "It was quite a trip," Charlie said, "My dad was on the woodpile with the rest of the crew, sawing away like crazy, to keep up the supply."

The White River got its name because of all the silt (and just plain mud) that it carries down from the glaciers. For the SS *Kluane* it was a matter of cleaning this silt from its boilers over and over again. They were six weeks making that trip, working their way upstream like a fish, until they got to Kluane Rapids, which was five or six miles below the lake. Their little sternwheeler came to a stop right there. Attempting to go any further meant never getting back out. So they kept blowing the whistles until the people at the lake finally heard them, and came with horse and wagons to pick up their freight and mail.

Taylor and Drury missed their bonus, but at least they had the satisfaction of delivering their load to the recipients. To Charlie's knowledge, the *Kluane* was the only steamer to ever go up the White River.

"My brother, Bill, and I would use any excuse we could, to get on the riverboats, when we were twelve and thirteen years of age," Charlie told us. "They used to give us jobs of painting the boat and the deck or the rooms. They didn't want us around the engines, but we always kept busy at something, and when we needed wood on those side rivers, we'd get out with the rest and cut it."

T & D had their own woodcamps on the main river, and hired a crew to work at these places. But on the side rivers the crew on their own steamboats had to stop and cut the wood, and pack it aboard the ship. Charlie and Bill really liked competing with the very capable Native boys when it came to this job, and they would go at it side by side—as fast as they could, two boys on each Swede saw, racing and hollering, and shouting to see who could get through first. "Bill and I didn't come in second very often," Charlie said, "because we were in pretty good shape."

In 1921, Livingston Wernecke came from Alaska and developed the Wernecke Camp, up on Keno Hill for the Alaska Treadwell Co. This caused a boom in the Mayo area, so Taylor and Drury established a store in Mayo, and another at Stewart City at the confluence of the Stewart and Yukon rivers, where thousands of sacks of ore from the mines were stockpiled on the banks. The large riverboats, on the way back from Dawson, picked this ore up, and took it to Whitehorse, where it was shipped outside for processing.

Coffee Creek was the next store to be established, just a few miles up the river from Stewart City. The freight required for all these stores became too much for their little ship *Kluane*, so T & D bought the steamer *Thistle* (which had been taken off the run by the White Pass) for very little money. They did a lot of restoration work, and bought a barge for her to push. From then on they were able to service all their stores much more effectively. They could push up to ninety tons with the *Thistle*.

Another store was opened in Keno City, then Champagne. The company, however, never did establish in Dawson City. In 1929 they had an offer of a building there, and began making all the plans. The Keno store was going to be replaced with the one in Dawson; the downpayment had been made when a telegram came up from the owner, saying, "There's a pile of lumber at the back of the building which wasn't included in the price. I'll have to charge you another $500." The two partners talked it over, and decided this was a bit too much, and they cancelled the deal.

"It was rather a blessing," said Charlie, "because shortly after this, the depression hit, and had we been in Dawson, I think we might have gone down with the rest of the people in Canada who had over-expanded, and found themselves caught by the depression. Possibly Taylor and Drury Company was saved by a pile of lumber!" The steamer *Thistle* eventually came to an unfortunate end in 1929. This is how Charlie described the event.

One day a bad storm came up on Lake Laberge, and the

Thistle was pushing a full barge on the way to Mayo. Jimmy Jackson, their much-valued pilot for so many years, had retired, and an inexperienced man was running the boat on an early morning shift. The post that held the barge broke, because it was pulling too hard. Instead of swinging the boat out in a circle, the pilot backed up against the storm. The water was so rough it went down the Pitman holes, and flooded the boat with water. With the heavy load on the barge, and such a rush of water going through, it just snapped the boat in half. Luckily no one was hurt. The crew climbed aboard the barge, and drifted to shore.

Charlie had the job of breaking the news to his father, and when he told him that the *Thistle* was a complete loss, Isaac said, "Did anyone get hurt?" When Charlie replied, "No, they were all saved," his dad said, "Good! Let's get drunk!"

They never carried insurance on boats, the price would have been astronomical. The cargo had all gone down. A lot of the stuff, however, came bobbing to the top. They fished enough out of the water to load on a small barge and take to Whitehorse, where they had a salvage sale which helped recover a small portion of what they had lost.

Charlie Taylor had been taught how to merchandise, ship goods and much more, by a very astute Scotsman by the name of Charlie Atherton, who was a long-time valuable employee of Taylor and Drury, in Whitehorse. "Another one," said Charlie, "was a fellow by the name of Eric Richards, who was head of our dry goods department, and was a very qualified tradesman. He showed me how to bolt up cloth and cut it properly, and he taught me about threads, so I had a good training from him. When they shipped me off to Mayo, this training really served a good purpose." (Author's note: Eric Richards was my father.) Charlie met Betty MacLennan in Mayo, and they were married in 1936.

After the boats were taken off the river, and most of the trade had come to an end, a lot of the trading posts had to be shut down, so Whitehorse, once more, became the main focus of the operation. This time, the Taylor and Drury sons were taking an active part in the operation and decision-making, but the elder founders of the company, Will and Isaac, still made the major decisions.

It remained that way until Mr. Drury died, on September, 23, 1953. Charlie remembers that day very well. "We were just getting ready to leave the store, and Will was sitting on the shipping counter, feeling fine and kidding the girls; saying goodnight to all the staff. Sunday morning pneumonia hit him, and knocked him out, just like that." His passing was the end of a forty-five-year partnership, and it must have been a hard loss for the Taylors, as well as the Drury family.

In appearance and nature, the two men were opposites. Isaac Taylor was a short little man, who was always ready with a short and snappy answer to everything. William Drury was a large, portly man. He had a reflective personality, and always thought things through, pulling on his pipe all the while, before giving his opinion on anything. It made for a good combination of personalities, and they had enjoyed each other's company right to the end.

Even after Will had passed on, Isaac went to the office every day until he died in 1959. He was one month short of ninety-five years old.

Charlie told us he remembered the day in 1944, when he first told his father he would have to release some of the business to the boys. Isaac had suffered a stroke, but wasn't ready to give up the job as boss, yet.

He said, "I can't stop...where would I fit into the scheme of things?" Charlie told him the store lacked a good haberdasher in men's clothing. Ike said, "You want me to be the manager of the menswear department?" It was just what he wanted to hear!

"We were eating breakfast at the time, and it wasn't two minutes, until he had his hat on and was down at the store. I was all shaken up because it was hard to talk like that to my father, who had been so good to us for all those years, and tell him he couldn't be in charge anymore." Charlie hurried down to the store to see what was going on, and found Ike, his sleeves rolled up, behind the counter in the menswear, rearranging everything—happy as a lark! And the boys had their new manager in the men's department.

"Important business decisions were always resolved between the families in a democratic manner," Charlie said. After a vote was taken, he became general manager of the mercantile business; Bill Taylor and Bill Drury went into the automotive division; Albert Taylor went out to Vancouver, as a buyer for the company, and made his home there.

Whitehorse is still full of Taylor and Drury exemployees. Charlie told us (back in 1978) that he ran into them often. "The finest friends I have here are people who have worked for me. I can't go down the street without meeting someone who used to work for us. Or their moms or dads, and quite often their grandparents were part of our staff. I think it's the tie that keeps my wife and I living here," he said.

Charlie Taylor passed away in Whitehorse, in January, 1992.

3

The Goulter Family

"Farewell," we cried to our dearests;
Little we cared for their tears.
"Farewell," we cried to the humdrum,
And the yoke of the hireling years;
Just like a pack of school-boys,
And the big crowd cheered us good-bye.
Never were hearts so uplifted,
never were hopes so high.

Robert Service

Ida May (Mack) Goulter was born in Minneapolis in 1893. She met her husband at 33 Point, five miles below Eagle on the Alaska-Yukon border, in the year 1905. They were married in 1909, and lived in Carmacks for the rest of their lives. She was going on eighty-five years old when we talked to her. She remembers the SS *Columbian* going up in flames on September 26, 1906. Five people were burned to death in that fire. She and others watched the sparks coming out of the smokestack, just before it blew up. Mrs. Goulter maintains that those sparks were the reason for the boat burning, even though the story goes that one of the crew men standing on the stern of the boat shot a rifle at a duck, and somehow this was the cause.

Ida May's father, Mr. Mack, came up in 1898, with his four brothers, and eight oxen. Along the way they caught up with

'Swiftwater Bill Gates' and Jack London. The Mack brothers stayed on the shores of Lake Bennett and whipsawed logs into lumber to be used in boats and barges for themselves and other travelers who were waiting to continue their journey to the gold-fields. They talked everyone they could into building barges instead of boats, because they were more effective for handling freight. The barges had much less trouble going through Miles Canyon and the rapids than the boats, of which many were overturned in the rough water.

The Mack brothers built themselves an especially large raft, having brought about twenty tons of supplies all the way from Minnesota. It had taken them from February until the following June to transport it over the trail.

They stayed at Bennett for a month, building boats, supplying lumber for the Anglican Church that was in the planning stages then, and helping people bring their supplies over the Chilkoot Pass with the oxen.

When they reached the head of Miles Canyon, they helped people shoot the rapids in their barges. They would then have to walk back up the shore to help the next one. During this period there was a tramline built on the shores of the canyon. It consisted of two wooden rails hewed out of trees and set into the ground for wagon wheels to run on. It certainly made things easier for some of the gold seekers. They could transport their canoe and supplies by horse and wagon, instead of braving that treacherous section of the river.

When Jack London left Bennett Lake, he picked up a young couple, Mr. and Mrs. Sands, whom he had met there. They wanted to go north, so he took them in his boat, all the way to Stewart Crossing. London stayed in an old, abandoned cabin at first, and he helped the young couple build a road-house in Stewart that winter. After that he stayed there.

Mrs. Goulter shatters an old myth that Jack London used to live in Dawson City. She claims he never did. She says he stayed in Stewart the whole time, where he wrote 'that little book' as Mrs. Goulter called it, titled *To Build a Fire*. Later, when he was out of the country, he wrote his famous classic *The Call of the Wild*.

When Mr. Sands died, London sent his widow a copy of the book; it was the first copy off the press.

In 1899, Ida May's father (Papa, she called him) wanted to go back home to Minnesota, after prospecting was over for the winter. Swiftwater Bill had a lot of gold by then, and it was decided that they would walk back out, and Mack would help him carry the gold. By the time they had walked over the ice to Little Salmon their packs were getting pretty heavy, and they decided to get some help. They asked a husky-looking Indian chap called Charlie Bill to go with them and carry a load. They had quite a job explaining just what they wanted him to do, as he spoke no English at all. But finally, by means of twigs placed 'just so' in the snow, and with the help of many gestures, they got him to understand. He signalled, yes, he would accompany them, and off they went.

They never carried tents; only had one blanket each, an ax, a gun and shells, some hardtack, moose jerky and dried fish. Every night they made a brush camp, composed of three walls made of spruce boughs about three feet high, the open part away from the wind, and a bed built up of the boughs as well.

(Mrs. Goulter said she had seen an Indian baby born in one of those brush camps. She said the mother had the baby without any help from anyone, and when she held the poor little thing up it was blue from cold and immediately a coating of frost formed all over its body, before she had time to wrap it in furs. As far as Mrs. Goulter knew it survived just fine. The weather was around -60°F at the time.)

The three men kept doggedly on, carrying heavy back-packs and scaling the Chilkoot Pass until they reached Skagway, and could continue in relative luxury aboard the coast steamships. When they reached Seattle, Mr. Mack parted company with the other two and took a different route for the remainder of his trip to Minneapolis.

A year later, in 1902, back again in Little Salmon, Mack and his brothers were cutting wood for the riverboats, when he ran into Charlie Bill who had gone 'out' on foot with him the previous year. They both recognized each other immediately. Mack often puzzled over what had happened to the fellow.

Wonder of wonders, he could now speak enough English to make himself understood. Little by little he told Mack and the boys the story of how he had come back to the Yukon.

Swiftwater Bill and Charlie had gone on as far as Chicago, and it was there that Bill left his companion in a hotel while he went to check out the night life. "You stay here and wait for me," he told him, "I won't be gone long, and we'll be on our way in the morning." Charlie Bill waited and waited for hours, but Swiftwater never showed up. Apparently the man loved to party, and he got in with a wild crowd of revellers in the bar, got drunk and stayed out all night. At one point Charlie had to use the bathroom, and never having seen a flush toilet in his life until he had reached Skagway, he was not used to them. He had seen the chain that hung down from the enamel water tank up on the wall, but didn't know what it was for. In Skagway he had just closed the lid and that was that. However, now he decided to pull on the thing to see what would happen. Swoosh!! Down came the water with a roar, scaring the poor fellow half to death. He began to pace the floor like a caged animal, certain that he was in some kind of White Man's trap. Soon he could stand it no longer, and he grabbed his empty pack, and went out in the hallway with only one thing in mind. He was going back home! Out in the hallway he found a stairway, leading down to what he recognized as a kitchen, because there was a stove, pots and pans and food. No one was around, so he crammed some food into his mouth, filled his packsack at the same time, and ran out into the night.

He walked and walked, using the stars for direction at night. In the daytime, when going through wooded areas he 'read the trees' by examining the bark for moss; a bushlore trick he had learned from his elders. His moccasins were worn to threads, and his feet sore and blistered, but he kept going, day after day, night after night. Finally he came to a place that was all grass and flatlands as far as he could see. (Mack thought the country sounded like the Dakotas, by the way Charlie described it, but no one knows for sure.)

He saw some men leaving a house, and trudging off to a field, where there was some machinery. After a while a woman

47

came out of the house, and shook out a cloth. The Indian mustered up enough courage to go over and knock on the door after she had gone back in. When the lady saw what condition his feet and clothes were in she took pity and gave him a meal and some of her husband's clothes and boots. Then she packed him a lunch and Charlie went on his way again.

By sheer instinct and bushlore, Charlie managed to keep on the right course. One day he came to a lumber camp, and watched the men working. When it came time for the crew to stop and eat, he followed them in, sat at the table and ate. As it turned out, he stayed the rest of the winter there. They gave him a job at the plant, and in the process he learned how to speak some English, enough to get by on.

In the spring, he was on his way again, by foot. This time though, he had a makeshift chart to go by, given to him by one of the men at the camp. He traveled endlessly on and on. There were times when he would come to a river and have to walk along the banks for many miles until he came to a spot that was narrow and shallow enough to cross. One of the areas he traversed sounded exactly like the Dease Lake area, when he later described it to Mack. He lived on grass, bugs and roots. Another time he found himself in the mountains (which Mack decided had to be the other end of the Pelly Mountains, over on the north Nahanni). Even though he'd never been there before, he was terrified, because he had heard of the 'Mountain Men' who were still on the warpath, and used to come over the mountain and fight with the other tribes, and steal the women from their camps. (Even in Goulter's time this had happened.)

He kept on, many times fighting off swarms of mosquitoes, until, at long last, he began to recognize the country around Pelly banks, and he worked around until he came to the MacMillan River, and down into the MacGundy River, and right into Little Salmon. It had taken him a whole year, but he made it. All the way from Chicago!

Haltingly, in his broken English, he told the Mack brothers about his journey, and piece by piece they were able to put it all together. It was an incredible story of unimaginable endurance. After that he was always referred to as "Chicago Charlie Bill."

In 1898, Mr. Mack made another trip home to Minneapolis, once again traveling the ice portion of the trail by foot. (Mrs. Goulter said he made that trip three different times.) Swiftwater Bill was in Dawson City then, courting a dance-hall girl by the name of Bertie Labelle, who was apparently very fond of eggs, as well as gold! He let it be known that he intended to buy up every egg in town, if she would marry him. It seems that there was another rich lovesick prospector in town, by the name of Crawford who wanted Bertie for himself. When he heard the news, he hustled around and bought up all the eggs in town before Bill got around to it. Bertie played hard to get and refused to marry either one of them. Mrs. Goulter said that Bertie did 'take up' with Swiftwater for a while though. She said they were "married...but not churched!" But it wasn't long before she left him, and he picked up with her sister, who also left him after a short time. Swiftwater Bill didn't waste any time carrying torches around, and soon he found another girl. His money didn't last much longer than his girl friends, and eventually he lost it all, and went back "outside."

In 1902, the Mack brothers built two houses, a couple of miles below Little Salmon, with the intention of bringing Mac's wife and two daughters, and Frank's wife and daughter up from Minneapolis to live with them. They sent the money for fares, which was $100 each at that time, and the preparations for the trip north began in earnest for the two women and their daughters. Mrs. Goulter says her mother sold all their beautiful furniture, and bought heavy clothes for the family, packed up everything she thought they could use in the wood camp, and gave away most of their good clothes to charity. They were all set to leave, when they got a telegram from the men: "Don't come yet—We're going to go prospecting to Kluane!" It was while the men were prospecting and mining in this area, she said, that they named two creeks, one of them the '4th of July' and the other 'Ruby.'

By the fall of 1903, the men had built two more cabins and the women received another telegram. It said, "Come now. All's ready." Her mother had bought all new furniture, by this time, but she sent a message saying, "We're coming this time, whether you want us or not!" So, the five of them set off on the long trek north.

Ida May Mack was just ten years old then. Somewhere along the way the two families got separated, and her Uncle Frank's family arrived at their destination in June—the others got to Whitehorse on the 25th of August.

During the last year, Frank's wife had developed tuberculosis, but she decided to make the trip anyway, so she could bring her daughter, Mandala, to Frank. She never expected to live very long, and the next spring she passed on.

Dr. G. D. Terence, a government geologist, arrived in Little Salmon soon after that, and he named two of the lakes close by; the larger one 'Mandala' and the other 'Frank.' Mrs. Goulter said she was just a little girl at the time, but she remembers how proud she felt that her cousin and uncle had lakes named after them. She said that those lakes are in such a lovely valley that it really should have been made into a park. "Our houses were below Eagle Rock, on a bench," she said, "and we built a trail over to those lakes. We went over there a lot in the summer."

Almost all the people who lived on the river cut wood for the steamships. A few were prospectors, and some raised mink and fox, and trapped in the winter months.

Every man who had a wood camp, had a contract with the White Pass for 200 cords of green wood, and fifty cords of dry wood. There were wood camps all along the river, sometimes only ten miles apart, between Dawson and Whitehorse. The larger ones hired extra men, which entitled them to larger contracts. Big Salmon had a very large camp, it probably had 1000 cords or more. It was run by Byer and Hendrickson. Another large wood yard was at Minto, run by 'Old Man Thomas.'

If a man couldn't fall a cord of wood, cut it up into four foot lengths, and pile it in one day, he couldn't make any money, because they only made $4.50 a day, and fifty cents of that went to the government as a stumpage tax.

The men piled the wood six-feet high, and built it up in tiers to dry. It had to be all used up by the boats before the wood-cutters would get paid from White Pass. But every fall the cheque would arrive, in time for them to get their winter's supply sent in before the boats stopped running for the season. Later, this policy was discontinued, and the men were paid when the wood was piled on the banks.

The Mack boys had a horse, and only cut wood in the winter time. In the summer months they went prospecting.

When the Mack family moved to Tantalus (Carmacks), they were the only people living there, except for the Robinsons that were running the old CD roadhouse, catering to the passengers going through on the stage. There was Ida May's father, mother and sister—her cousin Mandala, her uncles, and the odd prospector would show up now and then. The Northwest Mounted Police moved in a few years later, and then an anglican minister, Rev. Cecil Swanson, who came in 1914. When the prospectors came in, the Macks would invite them over and they would sit up all night singing songs.

"My father and his brothers had wonderful singing voices. It's such a shame we didn't have a way to preserve their singing," Mrs. Goulter said. "My father had a high tenor that was an octave above a second tenor. Can you imagine that? And my uncle Jean had a clear deep bass. My uncle Frank carried the air (that's the treble). He and my uncle Fred had a good voice too, but nothing compared to my father and my uncle Jean. What did we do for entertainment on the river? Well, that's what we did. We sang. Any woodcutters that were within five miles of our place, would come over Saturday evening and we'd sing all night long. We had no other music in those days.

"My uncle Frank used to be a cook at one time in a wood camp, and he would bake a big pile of cookies for the whole gang, and we ate cookies and sang until midnight. Then the men would walk home again, to wherever they came from.

"We had no communications where we were, but there was a telegraph operator and a lineman at Big Salmon and at

Yukon Crossing. The operator at Big Salmon was Jack Hope, and the lineman was called Whispering Smith. One time around Christmas, someone threw a party at Big Salmon, and they sent us an invitation by telling one of these linemen, who went all the way down to Tantalus to give the police the message. So a police officer harnessed up his dog team, and Mac harnessed his, and away we went. We had a great time.

"Sometimes the Indians would come in to town at Big Salmon, and I remember they arranged a show for us and we watched the traditional dances. I've never seen it since, but this time they decided to show us their original dances, and my it was nice, quite primitive but very nice! Then they put on a potlach for us. It wasn't time for a potlatch, but they had all pitched in and built a great big campfire. There must have been about twenty of us from Tantalus, I guess, and about 100 Indians had come in from other camps for the celebration. Well, they asked us to come up to the campfire, and each of us got a gift. One man reached into a big moosehide bag and brought the presents out. I got a bracelet, I'll never forget how proud I was over that—it was all white beads and it was just lovely! And he also gave me a picture frame and a brass ring with a green stone in it.

"It was very seldom that the women got a chance to visit the other camps. They were too busy. Just that one time. The men went more often, but it was always on business. We never met a girl or another white woman the whole time we were on the river.

"In 1900, an Indian guide had taken a woman, Florence Hill, and a man Scotty McIntyre, to stake a copper property up in the mountains, but they had let it expire. Uncle Fred went in 1902, and staked the same property. Then he let it run out and my Dad staked it in 1903, and held it for years. In 1904, he took my mother up over the mountains with a horse, and she staked a claim next to it. I still have that claim today," said Mrs. Goulter, "after all those years."

Mrs. Goulter never rode on a paddlewheeler until after she was married. The couple raised two girls and a boy in Carmacks, Helen, Anne, and Frank Jr.

Frank Goulter Sr. was the last living survivor of the Northwest Mounted Police, when we talked to him in 1978. He was born in 1877, and his 102nd birthday was just coming up.

Mr. Goulter had joined the British army, when he was a lad of eighteen. The first place he was sent as a soldier was Ireland, and from there he went to India and South Africa (during the Boer War). The army discovered, after some time, that he was color blind, so he was forced to take an honorable discharge even though his eyesight was excellent. He had served in the army for twelve years.

Somehow, he ended up in Calgary, Alberta, before the city of Edmonton even existed, and soon after that he joined the Northwest Mounted Police, and came to the Yukon.

"It was alright for me," he said, "Not for everybody though. You were cut off from any kind of doctors and things like that, but doctors never troubled me anyway." He told us that he came to the Yukon because he could double his salary there. He would be getting a dollar a day, instead of fifty cents. The first assignment he was sent on was to Minto, as the Governor General's escort. He went back to Whitehorse, and from there he was sent to Carmacks, called Tantalus at that time, in 1905.

The river was bustling with boats and people in those days. Mr. Goulter remembered the time the Five Finger Rapids had to be dynamited to make it safer for the steamboats to go through. "There used to be a nasty drop-off there," he said, "but they blew a lot of big rocks out which made quite a difference."

A fellow by the name of Archie Pike put a cable in along the wall of the rapids, where it was narrow and the current was strongest. He used to charge any boat that went through $20 to pick up the line and use that cable to guide themselves through the channel. Some boat owners would go to great lengths to avoid picking that cable up, and a few of them got into some real predicaments because of this.

While Mr. Goulter was on the police force he spent a lot of his time on a patrol boat on the river. Little Salmon was the main Indian village then. "Lots of Indians there," he said. "but nobody between Big Salmon and Hootalinqua at all."

There were four policemen in Tantalus, including Scottie Hume. They took turns patrolling the river.

Mr. Goulter quit the police force in 1908, and went trapping in the Hootchi country on an old trail which was built by the Canadian Development Company, before Goulter's time. The people there called it the 'CD Trail.'

"That trail really opened up the country," Mr. Goulter said. The old stage (horse-drawn sleds) used to come that way. The sleds came out a couple of miles north of Laberge, over to Montague, then on to Braeburn (which was called Hootchi then) and from there to the Nordenskiold River, where they took to the ice for four miles to Tantalus.

The first old roadhouse at Montague burned down in 1914. The fire also took out the big barn, and all the livestock. Later, the White Pass built another roadhouse there to replace it, and brought old Mrs. Miles in to run the place.

After he was married, Mr. Goulter started a mink ranch, and did very well until the "Big Fellas," as he called them came into the country from the United States. They were the Brown Brothers...all millionaires. They ruined the trapping for everyone. "They kept the damn fox prices down to lower than $24. I was doing just fine before that," Mr. Goulter complained.

The coal mine at Carmacks was staked by a man called Jim Vey. He didn't register it, so someone else took it over. It never turned out to be much good, but they started mining anyway; he got his son in from the outside, a pretty handy fellow, and they started shipping coal to other points.

Then the White Pass decided they might be able to use coal on the boats instead of wood. For a trip or two they made the *Casca* into a coal-burning boat. This never worked out because they couldn't get a hot, or steady enough fire to keep steam up. The coal was of a very poor quality, it would crumble and the coal dust made such a mess that it wasn't worth all the effort needed to continually clean it up. So they went back to wood again. Mr. Goulter remembers a fellow by the name of Ted, who was a stoker on that trip, he said he had a terrible time trying to keep up steam, the coal kept breaking up all the time—they barely made it at all, he said.

54

So the White Pass sent a crew down from Whitehorse, about a dozen men, to work the coal mine. They figured the coal could be used for other purposes. It was this crew that enabled Mr. Robinson, who ran the road-house at Tantalus, to make a good living. When they eventually gave up the mine and the crew left, Mr. Robinson left too, but not before naming the town Carmacks.

"It should have been left as Tantalus." Mr. Goulter said, "Carmack was never here. He'd left the country long before this place was ever settled. In Carmack's time there was nothing here. He either went out over the CD trail, or he went out by steamboat."

For a while they did have a school, Mrs Goulter said. Adele Sampson came down and taught for two winters here. By the time she left there were more missionaries here, and they taught the children, Indians and Whites together.

Mr. Goulter spoke up, "Old George Black tried to get a school here, but it didn't work. Not enough kids, was the excuse. What they did learn, they learned mostly by themselves," he said.

"We used to have a big garden here when we were able to take care of it," said his wife. "We had better food in those days than we do now. We had lovely canned stuff, cases of beet greens and cases of what they called Silver Prunes. My they were awfully nice. And big ten-pound cans of date butter and apple butter. We had no fresh stuff at all in the winter, everything was dried, except the fish and caribou. The caribou used to come through by the thousands, so we were never short of meat."

In 1978, the Goulters could think of nobody left in the country who had come up in 1905, besides themselves. "We wouldn't move anywhere else," said Mrs. Goulter. "Why would we? We're contented right here."

Mr. Goulter spent forty-one years in Carmacks before he went back to visit Whitehorse, 100 miles away.

4

The Retallacks

—•◆◆◆•—

Till the moon set the pearly peaks gleaming,
And the stars tumbled out, neck and crop;
And I've thought that I surely was dreaming, With the peace
o' the world piled on top.

Robert Service

Stewart City was established in 1883. There were several mining outfits, and about 200 miners working there. When the Klondike gold rush started, most of these men left Stewart and went on to the gold fields around Dawson.

Tom Retallack was transferred to Stewart City in 1943, to manage the Hudson Bay store, and to look after the fur trade. His wife Athol thought it was the most delightful place she had ever seen. Nothing like her first impression of the town of Whitehorse, which was teeming with what seemed like 30,000 U.S. troops passing through, and the streets were a "sea of mud." Their hotel reservations were laughed at, just like the authorization they had obtained for a charter flight to Stewart.

Tom had a pilot friend in Whitehorse, Harvey Johnson, and he and his wife took the Retallack family in while they waited for the next available charter. When they were finally airborne, Athol looked down over the town they were leaving and thought, "I never want to see that awful place again." In 1946, on their way outside she wouldn't even go out of the hotel when they got to Whitehorse. They went straight from the hotel to the train station, and caught the train to Skagway.

Stewart was a lovely island, lush and green, as only the lower river can be. It had been built up of fertile silt, and everything grew to a maximum size there. Long days of sunlight and the good soil produced a wonderful garden for the Retallacks. Tourists from the riverboats would sometimes ask if they could have a pansy to press, because they had never seen any before with blossoms that measured four and five inches across. "We grew everything there," said Athol, "beautiful vegetables and flowers. And besides that, it was a bird sanctuary! Heaven help anyone who ever thought of bringing a cat onto that island. The old timers had banned them years ago, and they wouldn't allow any squirrels there, either, because they would rob the bird nests. It was a lovely, gentle place to live."

Not so gentle in the spring, though, during the annual break-up of the ice. The earth would shake with the raw power of great chunks of ice smashing against the bank. Every year, more of the bank would wash away...and the island would be diminished by a few feet.

On one occasion, Athol remembered, the ice jammed just below the island, and everything backed up. The ice was level with the river bank, and the Retallacks had no place to go. Tom moved some mattresses and things upstairs in the store, and set up a stove, quite prepared to be flooded out of their home. One of the old-timers came along with some life jackets, which he draped over their fence. "Oh, come on," he said to them, "you can't expect to live forever, now can you? But we'll make a stab at it anyway!" Then the ice suddenly broke loose, and the water, ice and debris drained away like somebody pulling the plug in a bathtub. It was all sucked downriver, plunging and grinding along, great massive blocks pushing and piling up on each other, on the wild dash downstream.

"We had heard some of the tales the local men told, about having to cut the dogs loose, during a flood, because they'd be swimming on the end of the ropes that were tied to the dog houses, and they would have drowned otherwise."

The folks at Stewart City only got their mail once a month in the winter. After the last steamboat left in early October, they would have a long wait, until the ice froze over solid enough for the mail to be brought in from the Indian River country. Athol remembered standing at the window, looking way down the ice, imagining that every spot in the distance was a dog team on its way. Finally, one day it would actually happen, and that would be their only contact with the outside world for another month. "But sometimes, when the mail arrived, and we read about the problems happening all over the world, we'd wonder if it was really worth getting the mail, after all," she said. "Because really, we were as contented as could be, right where we were."

Tom and Athol had a little boy named Tommy, who was kindergarten age. Athol taught her son at home, he had a special 'schoolroom' and a desk, and regular hours, just like a real school. Athol also took endless correspondence courses herself. She had a true thirst for learning, which continued through her entire life. "I have always had a compulsion for studying things," she said. "And when Tommy ran out of story books, I would just write some for him." They taught him how to read. Every night Tom would sketch little pictures in a reader they were making for Tommy and Athol would write the text. It was all about a little boy who lived on an island in the north. "He just couldn't wait, the next morning, to get into his classroom and see what was in his reader. That kept us busy, and because he was alone, we made sure that he wasn't lacking in the social activities he would have had if we were living in town. We had parties, and ball games and Easter eggs, and valentines, and all the rest."

One winter the Burians were their only neighbors, and another winter it was the Barbers. Both families moved up-river, after a while, and during their last winter at Stewart City, the Retallacks were there alone. The trappers had all taken off for the winter, living along the traplines.

"Our home was lovely, even without electricity and water. We had a well, and a pump in the kitchen, and I have a mighty right arm from pumping that thing. It was a full, busy, happy life. Three enchanting years, is the only way I can describe it, looking back."

The Hudson Bay supplied first aid equipment, but in Stewart they never had the occasion to use them. "Maybe it was just the resiliency of youth—maybe it was the silent prayer of thanks we gave every night—that no accidents or illness had occurred. You had to have faith that God in His goodness, would take care of things, or I don't think you could have stood it," Athol said.

The Retallacks also looked after the official post office at Stewart that had been established during the gold rush era. Summers at Stewart were a busy time. The steamboats were loaded with tourists, and many of them got off to shop in the store, look around and ask questions. "Sometimes it would be like a stream of locusts, they'd be all over the store," Athol said. "And people from Dawson City would be traveling back and forth a lot in the summer months. They knew they'd have to stay put in the winter. A lot of women would rush in here, and grab up the silk stockings, because during the war, they couldn't get any. These were old stock that had been in the store for a long time, they didn't last long, I'll tell you. But we always enjoyed meeting people."

One time, the Retallacks were hosts to a stowaway who had been dropped off at Stewart by the captain of the paddle-wheeler, when he was discovered on board. The captain told Tom that the young man would be picked up there the next day, and taken to the police in Whitehorse. He seemed like a rather surly fellow, who couldn't look them in the eye. They fed him and put him in a guest cabin that Tom had built for company who might be staying overnight. "We'd never had a stowaway before," said Athol, "and I was extremely nervous." Midnight came, and she was lying awake, too uneasy to sleep, so she asked Tom if he'd just go out and check up on the fellow in case he was prowling around or something. Tom got dressed, and went out to see. In a very short time, he was back, grinning all over his face. "I went down to that cabin," he said, "and hammered on the door, and a scared shaky voice cried, 'Who is it...who is it?'" He said it took about ten minutes to take down all the barricades that young fellow had erected around the door. He was afraid that the bears and wolves would be after him. So Tom reassured him that he'd be safe, and they both went back to bed. When morning came they gave him breakfast, and later in the day a steamboat stopped by and picked him up. "That was the only overnight guest that I wasn't sure of," said Athol.

Both Athol and Tom became radio operators while they were at Stewart. The telegraph line came through there, and after the telegraph operator left in the spring of 1946, they had the line hooked up to their radio phones in the house. This way they could maintain contact with Dawson, by tapping out Morse code messages. "You could tap it out on a phone, if your voice contact wasn't working, or if there was too much static on the line. It was all code then. Incidentally, I can still read and tap it out, fairly rapidly. Guess it's like riding a bike, you never forget how."

Athol loved the cold, still winter nights, brightened by the moon on the snow, or the northern lights. "I have actually heard the northern lights," she said, "It's so still, you can hear them going...swish, swish. They really light up the sky, and they're so beautiful. And the colder the night, the brighter the stars are." Tom and Athol used to take turns stoking up the wood furnace in the store, during the coldest nights, when it would get around -60°F. They couldn't take a chance on things freezing over there, so every three hours they would take turns going over to toss some four-foot logs into the furnace. "There was something exciting about doing that," Athol said, "I don't know just what it is, but it's something to do with the stillness, and the quiet, and the being out there all alone in the middle of the night; hearing the coyotes howling, or a frozen tree snapping in the cold, knowing that your family is safe and warm in the house, with smoke from the chimney billowing straight up into the sky.

"We never had the need for anyone else. We had each other and that's all that really mattered. We never lost that closeness, and I think a lot of it is due to those years together at Stewart City."

5

The Camerons

―――・・◆・・―――

Ahead of the dogs ploughed Clancy,
Haloed by steaming breath;
Through peril of open water,
Through ache of insensate cold;
Up rivers wantonly winding,
In a land affianced to death,
Till he came to a cowering cabin,
On the banks of the Nordenskiold.

Robert Service

Gordon Cameron was born in Three Rivers, Quebec in 1900. He was living in Vancouver, B.C., where he was a member of the Northwest Mounted Police, when he got a call from the Sergeant Major, at ten o'clock one morning, saying, "You'll be going to the Yukon, and your boat will leave at five o'clock."

He didn't take long to get ready. "Just threw my shaving kit in a bag, and away I went," said Cam. "I'd heard a lot about the Yukon, in the past few years, and it was something to look forward to."

He married Martha Ballentine, of Dawson City, and the couple moved to Fort Selkirk in 1935, and made it their home until 1949. They raised their daughter, Ione, in a cabin on the banks of the Yukon River. There were about fifteen white people living in Fort Selkirk, and around ninety Natives; men, women and children, in the nearby vicinity, when they weren't away, trapping, hunting or fishing.

There were two stores, Taylor and Drury, and the Hudson Bay Company; two mission schools, the Roman Catholic and the Anglican, for the Indian children; and of course there was the ever present, and essential, telegraph operator. The Indian children came and went with their parents in those days, so they got their schooling in "fits and starts."

Gordon I. Cameron, was the officer in charge of the RCMP barracks. Martha enjoyed the life at Fort Selkirk. "Every day we would be outside, regardless of the cold in the winter. We'd just bundle up and go right out in it. I remember one time—it was eighty-six below zero, and the Hudson Bay manager's wife and I went out for a walk, just to say we could. Mind you, we dressed up well, and we went out to the airport and back. There's not that much difference between forty below and eighty, you know. You just have to cover your mouth up better, but when you're all bundled up like that, there's very little difference. That's just for a very short time, of course."

But when it got that cold the Camerons nailed blankets over the doors, and brought wood in only once a day, in order to keep out the cold blast of air that would rush in when the door was opened. They would have to empty the ashes in the heater once a day, too, because a lot of wood was thrown in the fire in twenty-four hours, when the mercury dipped that low.

The men were away a lot. "Cam" would be gone on a patrol of the river, with his dog team, and there were four trappers' wives in the village, whose husbands spent a good deal of time on the traplines. "The women didn't mind this at all," Martha told us, "we used to play cards. Whoever was baking bread that particular night, everybody would go to that home, and play canasta, or whist. We were never lonesome.

"It wasn't like it is today, either. When a mountie left home you wouldn't hear from him for two to three weeks, or maybe a month. You'd have an idea of the general direction he went in and that was it. It was just a life that you got used to. It was kind of a pleasant thing to have the old man away for a few weeks at a time," laughed Martha.

When Ione reached school age, she was sent 'outside' to a boarding school. Martha took on the contract to saw all the wood for the barracks. The police bought the wood in four-foot lengths from a wood cutter, and she cut it in sixteen-inch lengths. Later on, when the airstrip was put in, she got the contract to keep it rolled. She had a two-ton Caterpillar tractor, and a little roller. "I was allowed to keep my own hours," she said, "So I worked every day at it, in the winter. I loved to be outside and keep myself active." She got a dollar and a half an hour.

Fort Selkirk was not much of a garden spot. They grew good rhubarb, but not much else. In the summer, the women picked berries and made their own jellies and jams. One year Martha had 365 jars of wild fruit. When the OC (officer in command) came in one time, he told the Camerons, "Well, we can't transfer you people. We couldn't afford to transfer all that fruit!"

In the winter months the folks at Fort Selkirk got together and cut blocks of ice from the river, which were stored in a cabin that was filled with sawdust. They buried the ice in the sawdust where it would keep all summer long.

Visitors used to come to see them often, in small boats, and in the winter a lot of planes would get stranded there, due to the weather. "We had fifteen passengers one time, on a plane that had flown from Texas, and was on its way to Alaska," Martha said. "They were stuck down here for about five days. Everybody took someone in, and at night we'd have a good pow-wow, and a sing-song. In the morning I'd get a thermos and lunch ready for them to take on the trip. They'd take off, then find out they couldn't get over the pass, and they'd be back. This went on for four days, and then Fred Boss came over. He was down here on the SS *Hazel B* working on the airport. We had him over for the evening, and he made 'medicine' for them. The next day they took off without any trouble. He knew what to do, old Fred."

In the fall, towards the end of the season, when it got dark, the steamboats would sometimes tie up at Fort Selkirk for the night. "We'd have a real party at the house on those nights." Martha said.

The trappers used to pole up the river, they didn't have outboard motors on their boats, and sometimes they would pole all the way up to Minto from Fort Selkirk. Other times they went up the MacMillan River, and trapped there. A few of them would spend their summers up the MacMillan. "I've gone up there myself, a few times," said Martha. "I spent two weeks there one summer, with a family. We had a marvellous time. We'd go up into the mountains where the glaciers were, just to get ice for our ice cream. Took us all day to go in there, and backpack that ice out. There were four of us, and by the time we got back to camp, there was just enough ice that hadn't melted to make our ice cream."

When the U.S. Army came in during the war, they sent a bunch of men to Fort Selkirk, to survey up and down the river. About sixty men camped out just behind the police barracks. Martha had a few gold nuggets, and she'd put some of them in a gold pan, and pretend she'd just found gold in the river. It is what the sourdoughs call, 'salting' a pan. The soldiers from the camp out back, would come over to see what she was doing, and get really excited. They rushed over to the store and bought up all the gold pans they had. Once in a while Martha would manage to plant a little nugget in somebody's pan.

"We had some good times between ourselves, at Fort Selkirk," she said, "We had to make our own entertainment, and that's just what we did. I was never lonesome once, in all those years, even when Cam was away on patrol. When the depression came, we never felt it at all. We knew it was there, but it didn't touch us."

Cam used to make furniture out of banana crates, or gas cases. Gas used to come in wooden boxes, with two five-gallon cans to the box, they were useful for furniture and cupboards. Nothing that could be used ever went to waste.

Martha: "My chesterfield was two steamer trunks with lots of prison blankets on top. I made fancy cushions for it, and our cabin was really nice, and quite attractive."

When someone was sick in the village, Martha would attend to them. She delivered babies, gave shots with a needle, when necessary, and generally performed the duties of a health nurse.

"The first time I had to give someone a shot," she remembers, "I thought to myself...should I have someone in to help me, or should I go it alone." She decided to go it alone because if she made a mistake, no one would get blamed except her. That man told her it was the best needle he'd ever had. She gave out medicine and bandaged up small wounds. If it was a case beyond what she or Cam could handle, they would have to telegraph for help. Once the airstrip was in, they could just charter a plane and send the injured person out to Whitehorse for further aid. The government would look after expenses in those cases.

"Cam put a finger back on a guy once, sewed this old Indian fellow up, and he's still living. He had caught it in the engine of his outboard motor. He holds his hand up when he sees Cam now, and says, 'Here's the finger you put back on!'"

One young fellow was chewed up badly by some dogs, and Cam and Martha shaved off his hair and sewed up his scalp. "You had to do it," Martha said, "what else could you do? There's no one but you to turn to. Before the airplanes came, there was one thing for sure, if I didn't heal them, Cam would bury them!" They never had much trouble at all. Everyone seemed to heal nicely, and no one ever got infection from any of their stitching. Martha thought that being out in the bush, where pollution was unknown in those days, gave you a sort of immunity from infection and germs.

In the fourteen years they were in Fort Selkirk the turnover in ministers was very small, only four changed locations. Among the ones living there were Reverend Chappell, Reverend Bob Ward, Bishop Stringer's son, Randall Stringer, and a chap by the name of Robertson. Mrs. Cowaret was the schoolteacher. She had been an anglican missionary, before marrying a trapper, and had made her home in Fort Selkirk.

In the winter time there was not a great deal of travel. One year, two dog teams came all the way from Dawson, but that was the only time anyone had come from that distance. The mail came down from Minto by dog team, where it had been dropped off by the overland stage. Fort Selkirk had a regular money order post office, with numbered mail boxes for everyone. This was unusual for a village on the river. In order to maintain it, they had to have a certain number of stamp sales. The postmistress used to send all her friends postage stamps for Christmas, so she could keep the sales up. Everybody uses postage stamps, she thought, so what better present could you give?

"It was very lonely for the people at the wood camps in the winter," Martha said. "As soon as the ice was out we'd go down and have a drink of rum with a fellow by the name of Marshall, and he'd be so glad to see us." Of course Cam patrolled the river all winter, so he'd see most of them at some time or another.

Martha never went to Minto very often, although it was the nearest community. Once though, she had to have a bad ear attended to, and she took her dog team over the ice to Minto, and caught the overland stage to Mayo. She arrived in Mayo that same day. "So it wasn't any problem," she said.

"Even though we weren't lonely, it was kind of nice to see the first steamboat arriving in the spring," she told us. They always enjoyed the fresh fruit, meat and vegetables that the boat brought, seeing the new faces among the passengers, and the familiar ones of the captain and crew.

The last boat was the one they enjoyed most, though. The village folk would show up at the wharf in their best clothes, and if the boat overnighted, as they often did, there would be a grand going away party. But it was sad to see them leave the next morning, just the same, knowing that it would be many months of cold winter, before they would see them again.

Martha told us that most of the cabins in the village were built by Afe Brown and Alec Coweret, many, many years ago. Afe raised his family there, and the house that the Camerons lived in had once been his home. He had sold it to Schofield and Zimmerlee, who, in turn, used it for a home while they were building a store there. In the late 1930s, the Hudson Bay

Company had come in and bought them out, along with all the cabins in the near vicinity. The Camerons home was rented from the Hudson Bay during their years in Fort Selkirk.

At Christmas time, all the families decorated a spruce tree and cooked a turkey. Each night they would go to a different home for dinner, until the last of the turkeys were consumed. The wives always cooked a lot of extra food, and all the single men were welcome to come and join in the festivities. Ione Cameron would usually be there for the holidays. They would dress her up as Santa Claus, and Martha and the Hudson Bay manager's wife, (who was a tiny little thing, Martha said) were Santa's elves. They took one dog on the sleigh, and went around and delivered goodies to every single man who was in town.

During an extremely cold spell one winter in February, a cabin caught fire. It belonged to a little old man, who lived by himself on the outskirts of the village. Cam was away at the time, and Martha went over to help the others fight the fire. As the logs went up in flames it soon became apparent that they weren't going to save the cabin. They stood there watching it burn, throwing junk back into the fire, as bits and pieces flew off. The roof began to collapse, and as Martha watched, a box came sliding off, and fell to the ground. It was the box of cookies and goodies that she had given him for Christmas! "Why, that old so-and-so," she thought. He had told her how he had enjoyed every one of them. And here was the box, quite intact; he had never eaten one cookie or chocolate...so she just threw it in the fire with everything else.

The next day he came over to Martha's house with tears in his eyes and said, "Someone stole my box of goodies." Martha said, "I thought you ate them." The old man said, "They were too pretty to eat. It was the very first time in my whole life that anyone had given me anything nice. I used to take it out every night and look at it, and then I'd put it back again." So Martha had to get busy and make him another Christmas box, in February, to make up for the one he lost in the fire.

"We had pretty Christmas trees." Martha said, "Every year I'd go and cut my own, and Cam would take movies of me. We made our own decorations, except foil and tinsel, which we bought. We had paper snowflakes, and popcorn strings, and we cut pictures and scenes from last year's Christmas cards. Made cardboard rings to hang them up, and chains out of colored paper. We had no electricity for lights, but nobody missed it. And I never believed in candles on a tree. As far as our lighting went, kerosene, and Aladdin lamps worked just fine."

G. I. Cameron—His Story

Whitehorse was the head of navigation on the Yukon River in the time that Constable Cameron was transferred to the Yukon. The White Pass had their offices there in the train station, and a big dock facility directly behind that, with warehouses stretching along the river bank a quarter mile to the shipyards. In the early days their whole outfit had been located at Canyon City, which was just above Miles Canyon, two miles up river from Whitehorse. When the railway was built, there was no need for the boat traffic from Lake Bennett to the Canyon, so the White Pass Co. moved to Whitehorse.

The police had the mail run to Dawson in those days. They ran over the ice on the Yukon River with dog teams. After the police gave up the mail, it went out for contract to the general public. Upper Laberge, 30 miles below Whitehorse, was an important police post during Cam's early days in the country. It had replaced the old Tagish post, which was always the main one before the railway was built. All the boats going downriver from Lake Bennett had been checked through at that post, and registered. Cam was able to make use of the White Pass steamboats for his patrols in the summer months.

Often, when the paddlewheelers were crossing Lake Laberge, a wind would blow up. In extremely rough water, you could actually see the deck rippling on those flat-bottomed boats, and when they worked with the waves like that there was always a danger of the steam pipes breaking, so they would have to tie up, and wait for the wind to die down. "Those ships were not made for heavy seas," said Cam.

The skippers had a river chart, which was kept on a round

cylinder, and could be unrolled as they went along the river. It was advisable to use it, Cam said, especially at night. Of course when traveling at night they also had big search lights, that could be trained on the markers which the captains and skippers had previously placed at strategic spots along the shore, on the sandbars, and even hanging from trees in some cases. Each spring these markers and charts would be altered because the river channels changed from year to year. Markers made from barrels or rocks painted white were commonly used.

"Little Salmon was an Indian village. There was a Taylor & Drury post there for a while, and an Anglican mission with a residence for the minister. Bob Ward, was the last one there, in the early 1940s, I believe. Most trappers brought their fur into the post there. Some people talk a lot about how the trappers were robbed, but they weren't really. You never heard of a trader getting out with much money. They bought the fur mostly on spec, you know. They didn't know what the fur prices would be by the time the buyers outside got the shipment, so they had to have a fair margin to work with. Sometimes they bought up a bunch of fur, and the market dropped right off...and they'd be left holding the bag. But they never turned a man down, no matter who he was. Even a ninety-year-old man could always get a little piece of jaw-bone. (This was the term for credit in those days.) They kept the trappers going that way, if times got hard they knew they could always get something."

G. I. Cameron patrolled the whole river from Whitehorse to Dawson, and the side streams as well, such as the Pelly and Stewart rivers. In his years at Selkirk, he used the police boat, and whenever he could, the paddlewheelers, in the summertime.

At Ogilvie Island, at the mouth of the 60 Mile River, lived a fellow by the name of Cruikshank, who had one of the few big farms on the river. He raised hay and oats there, and occasionally he came into Dawson to sell his fresh produce to the stores. The thing Cam remembered about him most was his wonderful rhubarb patch. He had a specially made rhubarb wine, and whenever Cam stopped by, on one of his patrols, he'd say, "Cameron, I've been saving this rhubarb wine, just for you!" He had a pail there in the kitchen, that he used for milking the cow, which was at this time, half full of garbage and potato dust. He would say to Cam, "Just grab that pail over there, and when I open this bottle, you catch it, 'cause it's pretty active." He would pull the cap on one of the bottles, and Cam would hold the pail underneath, until it quit squirting. "It was sure skookum stuff!" Cam said, "Two of those bottles, and I'd go down the river, singing to myself."

"Coffee Creek was an old established location that went right back to the Russian times; an old chap farming there had turned up pieces of copper, metal, brass and beads that were definitely of Russian origin. Goes right back to when the Russians owned Alaska. It was always a central meeting spot for the Indians. There was an old mountain trail, that was a crossing point for the Indians and Russians for many years. It went west from Coffee Creek and over to Alaska. There was farming going on there for many years, also."

One summer, after Mr. Cameron had retired, he and Cal Waddington went on a river trip together, and at Ogilvie Island they went exploring for any signs of the early trading post that Leroy McQuesten and Al Mayo, had put in there. There was still the outline of the old building left; it was built around 1886. McQuesten and Mayo used to go down to St. Michael in the spring in one of the first riverboats on the river, Cam said. They took as many people as they could with them, and they all cut wood and prospected along the way, and made a summer vacation out of it, because it took all summer to get there. Then in the fall they would come back with the winter supply of staples. That was before Dawson City was established.

In the winter months, Cam and his dog team usually patrolled the Pelly river alone, and he went right down the Stewart River. There was no point in going any further downstream, because the Dawson-Stewart run was a well-packed trail, looked after by the Dawson police.

Cam would generally get away in March, and head up the MacMillan, and Pelly rivers. "I'll see you in a month," he'd say to Martha, and she would wave goodbye, as he jumped on his dog team and took off. There were no trails on this beat. He traveled over snow-drifts and river ice to get to his destinations, taking the mail to the trappers along the way. Cam would be the only soul most of them would see all winter in those isolated spots. He was always most welcome at all the camps. "There were many times," he said, "When you'd arrive tired and hungry, after traveling all day, and the first thing the trapper did was bring out a bottle of rum. He'd be ready to talk your head off, when really, all you wanted to do was sleep! They wanted to hear all the news, and you couldn't really blame them at all."

In later years, Cam gave up keeping dogs himself and hired a team from one of the men in the village, and the two of them would go on patrol together. "We used to put on weight in the summer months," Cam said, "just sitting in the canoe, going down river. We'd hop a steamboat to come back up, and it was a pretty easy life. We soon took off those extra pounds running after the sled in the winter time."

The police made their patrols by boat right up until the time the ice formed, and then they knew right where everybody could be found in the winter. They handled all the Territorial Government work along the river, inspections, wood contracts and whatever else came up, and they made sure that no one was wanting for medical supplies or services. "We pulled the odd tooth out, and did whatever needed to be done. It was just a regular procedure. We had the tools to do the job, but no anesthetics, though. There were times we'd come in to a camp, and someone would say, 'I've got a bad tooth here,' and we'd go right to work on it. 'This is going to hurt you more than it will me,' we'd tell them. Nobody backed down; some of them thought twice when they saw me getting out my tools, but they went through with it."

Once in a while they would have a broken leg or arm to contend with, but not very often. Those woodsmen were very tough, but also very careful, they knew how to take care of themselves. And they didn't take chances; it was a matter of survival. In extreme cases they would have to take someone out of the bush to a center where they could get additional first aid until they could catch a boat to town, and after the planes started landing at Selkirk, they would be sent in to the hospital that way. Sometimes Cam would have to bury people. Most of them died of natural causes, and it was to be expected, and accepted, that they would be buried in their natural surroundings.

It was sometimes a source of worry for the family, if Cam was late returning from a patrol. One time, he told us, he was a whole week overdue. It was a terribly cold, windy night, and his little daughter, Ione, looked up at her mother and said, "Mommy, I wonder if the coyotes have got Daddy, this time."

The Departments of Forestry, Fisheries, and Game were handled by the police in Whitehorse, up until 1949, and often when a police officer was ready to retire from regular service, he transferred to an office in one of those departments. By the time the 1950s rolled around, the fishery and forestry departments were no longer under the RCMP jurisdiction, but had become government branches in their own right.

The Camerons moved out of Selkirk in 1949. Cam had put in his time with the police force, and was ready to retire from that job, so they moved to Whitehorse, where he went to work for the Territorial Game Department. The work was much the same as that which he had done while in the police force. He was assistant director of game and publicity.

A policeman by the name of Hall was sent to Selkirk to take Cam's place. When the Dawson and Mayo roads were completed in 1952, the highway came close to Minto and bypassed Selkirk. That was when the remainder of the people there packed up and left. Most of the Indian families moved to the Pelly Crossing, where the road went through...and that was the end of Selkirk. At that time the old telegraph line was also abandoned. The RCMP post was moved to Minto, and later on to Carmacks, where it remains to this day.

Once the paddlewheelers were taken off the run, everybody along the river moved out, except for the odd family or woodcutter, here and there. The Taylor and Drury trading posts all closed down, the Hudson Bay closed, and even the mission schools moved out. There was no reason to be there anymore.

Cam: "This country grows on a person, I've known people who have lived in a city all their lives, that have come up here and took to it right away. Some of them have never looked back. You couldn't make them leave now if you tried. And others who have been born here, can't wait to get outside and get away from it all. It all depends on a person's temperament. I've always loved the country, and I'm still with it.

"The river's full of old ghosts today, you go along in a boat with someone and ask, 'Does old Frank still live here now?' and they laugh and say, 'Oh, he's been gone for a long time. So and so?...Well, he's buried up here on the bank...and old Joe—he died long ago.' And that's the way it goes now. I guess that's a natural thing, when you get to be my age. You don't hear the sound of the old paddlewheels any more, or the steam whistles blowing. It's all gone.

"There's new people coming now. The old communities are gone, yes, but you go down that river today, and there's all kinds of boats on it. Canoes, kayaks, rubber rafts, dozens of them. They'll find the river again."

(As of this writing, Cam, as he is lovingly called by all his many friends, is still living in Whitehorse. His daughter, Ione, the little girl who was raised on the banks of the Yukon River, is also living there with her husband, after putting in a stint as Commissioner of the Yukon Territory, and also as mayor of Whitehorse. Both G. I. and Ione are members of the Order of Canada. Martha Cameron passed away May 29, 1990.)

6

Chappie Chapman's Story

———•••◆•••———

The snows that are older than history
The woods where the weird shadows slant;
The stillness, the moonlight, the mystery,
I've bade'em goodbye—but I can't.

Robert Service

Charles H. Chapman was born in 1902 in Essex, England. He came to Canada at a very young age, and lived in Maple Creek Saskatchewan, until he was eighteen years old. He joined the Royal Northwest Mounted Police, and was sent to the Yukon in 1920, where his first job was that of 'teamster.' He was assigned a team of black horses, and his duties were to oversee and haul prisoners around, and to haul wood and water to all the buildings in the 'barracks square' including the officers' quarters.

"Whitehorse was pretty small in those days, there wasn't much north beyond what is now Steele St. and down towards the other end of town which was Lambert Street," he said. "You were right into the woods from there on. There were around 300 people in town at that time. Of course when the boat crews and repair crews began arriving in the spring, there would be more, until the fall of the year when they'd all leave again."

In 1921, Chappie opened a police detachment at Ross River. "I went downriver on a small boat called the *Thistle* which was operated by Taylor and Drury. They had many branches along the Yukon River, one at Champagne, Carmacks, Fort Selkirk, Teslin and Ross River. I remember when we booked our tickets on that boat, being told that passengers were expected to get off and help cut wood, because there were no wood camps on the Pelly River. So we got out and cut wood. Bishop Stringer was a passenger also this time, and he and I both got on opposite ends of a cross-cut saw. It felt good to be off the boat for awhile. It took about four days to get to Ross River. There were no chain saws and very few Swede saws in those days. So most of the wood was cut with these big four-inch and six-inch cross-cut saws."

There was a big sign on the store at Ross River, it was called Nahanni House. It was the closest trading post to the Nahanni, the next closest was Lower Post. There were no roads anywhere then. The Indians would come over from the Nahanni, and buy their provisions for the whole year from the store, then they'd just disappear. Chappie spent a whole winter just traveling up the Pelly, and over Frances Lake, with a team of four dogs, visiting all the people who were living there.

In 1920, there were quite a number of steamboats operating on the Yukon River in the summer months, the *Klondike, Casca, Whitehorse, Canadian, Dawson* and the *Aksala,* as well as the *Thistle.* In the fall, the steamer *Yukon* and the *Alaska* would come up from the lower river at Tanana on the Alaska side, and winter at Whitehorse. Most of the wood for these boats was being hauled out to the river banks by horses. Caterpillars were starting to come then, a few old gas Cats (model 30s) replaced the horses on the stage line on the Dawson Trail.

Chappie stayed with the police until he had finished his service in August 1928, and then went to work for the White Pass as checker on the dock. He checked all the freight that came in on the train, and supervised the loading of it onto the boats.

When he tired of that job, he went to Mayo where he met a fellow by the name of Tommy Kerruish. The two men operated a diamond drill for the International Diamond Drill Company of San Francisco that summer and then went back to

Whitehorse. They drilled at a mine just above the Kopper King mine, the Pueblo mine, and the War Eagle mine. Then the company pulled out of those spots, as they were not considered rich enough to open up again. They had all operated during World War I, and were closed again, right after the war ended.

Their next adventure was joining a stampede to Squaw Creek. They went up the old wagon road to Champagne Landing, then up the Dezadeash River in a small boat, crossed Dezadeash Lake, and then took packhorses in to Squaw Creek. They were only there a short time, because Tom Kerruish didn't like the area. The pay dirt was far too deep, and the boulders unsurmountable, he thought.

The next year they went on a prospecting trip up the Hootalinqua River (now called the Teslin River). They worked up there most of the summer, prospecting on a sandbar called the O'Brian bar. They saw the remains of the old steamer *Norcom*, which is still there, at the confluence of the Yukon and Hootalinqua rivers. It used to belong to the Northern Commercial Company and it ran on the lower river. It was renamed the *Evelyn* at a later date.

The White Pass always wintered one of their smaller boats at Lower Laberge, either the *Keno*, the *Canadian* or the *Nasutlin*, and every spring they would run an old gasoline-powered tractor, with a steering wheel in the front, down the ice from Whitehorse to the boat. The tractor pulled a big sleigh, that was loaded with nonperishable goods, which were in short supply in Dawson City. The goods were loaded onto the steamboat, and sent downriver almost a month before any of the other boats could get through the ice at Lake Laberge. (The old tractor finally went through the ice in Bennett Lake.)

The White Pass tried different schemes to get the ice moving earlier in that lake, but most of the methods they tried didn't work. They tried spraying lamp black on it in the early spring, when the sun would heat it, and it did work fairly well. But the main thing that would move that ice was the wind, after the ice started to break up. There was a dam, just south of Whitehorse at Marsh Lake, that was built for the purpose of washing the ice out of Lake Laberge. It would hold the water back, until late in May, when they would let all the water go at once, to raise the water and flush away the ice.

There was a kind of bottle-neck at the entrance to Lake Laberge, where it would build up with silt, and that always caused the boats problems as well. They used to send a steamboat up there, and by turning the paddlewheel backwards and forwards, it would act as a dredge to clear the silt out of the channel.

The 30 Mile used to be a very difficult piece of river, but later on they had a lot of the rocks blasted out at the mouth, which made navigation much easier.

The river boats on the Yukon were totally dependent on the wood camps, which were situated every twenty miles apart, usually at the mouth of a stream. When the boats were pushing heavy barge loads of ore they would have to stop often to take on wood.

The smaller steamboats that ran on the Stewart River, the *Nasutlin* and *Keno*, brought the ore down from Mayo and Elsa. Elsa was called the Wernecke Mine at that time. The ore was loaded on the shore at Stewart City, (where the Stewart joins the Yukon River) and picked up by the larger boats that were pushing almost empty barges, on their way back upstream to Whitehorse.

After his prospecting venture, Chappie went back to Mayo looking for a job, and met Kippy Boerner. Kippy was a riverboat captain, and a part owner in the Northern Commercial Company (NC). Chappy started working for him, and was put in charge of the NC store in Mayo. He stayed there until 1933, at which time he was transferred to their store in Dawson City.

"The NC was an old established company in the Yukon and Alaska. They had opened their store in Dawson in 1897, I think, and they had some thirty or forty branches all over Alaska, from Nome right through to Anchorage, at Fairbanks and all along the river...Fort Yukon, Circle City and Eagle. I worked for them for over twenty years."

His main job in Dawson City was that of accountant for the company, and later he was put in charge of the whole opera-

77

tion. The big thing was to supervise the ordering of supplies—they carried groceries, hardware, clothing, mining supplies—and make certain the order was large enough, and have it all landed in Dawson before the river froze over in the fall. For many years the NC was the only grocery store in Dawson. They would have to order enough groceries for the whole community, as far as Old Crow, 60 Mile and 40 Mile. It was all brought down from Whitehorse by the riverboats. (The expression 'down from Whitehorse,' seems strange, considering that one travels 'up north to Dawson,' but due to the fact that the boats ran downstream on the river to get there, 'down from Whitehorse' becomes the appropriate way of describing the route.)

The main store took up a whole city block. They owned a group of huge warehouses, and had their own loading dock on the river. (The old curling rink, that was used up until the 1970s, was originally an old NC warehouse, that was used for beer storage. In the early days the NC sold beer, wine and whiskey.) They had a little railroad, that came from their dock through one of the warehouses on front street—back of what is now the Palace Grand Theatre, and then over to King Street, and up to the warehouses back of the curling rink.

When Chappie was there, the company had trucks hauling their supplies, but in the early days they used that railroad with small carts on the tracks, and a horse pulling them. They could haul a ton of flour in each cart.

The NC also had a big steam boiler plant on the river-front right there in Dawson, and that served as the fire protection for the equipment.

Up as far as the Pearl Harbour Hotel (which burned down later), and back of the Palace Grand, there was a tunnel under the street. You could actually walk in this tunnel—it was six-feet high. The water mains and steam heating mains were kept in there to keep them from freezing.

A lot of the woodcutters were very reliable people, and the NC used to ship in double-compressed bales of hay and oats for horse-feed. These people had permission from the company to take what they needed off the boats, and the NC would bill them for it later. Everything was done on credit, or jaw-bone, when Chappie first went there. People would even charge their groceries, and pay for them when the dredges started up in the late spring. The year 1933 was the height of the depression days. Prices of all commodities had dropped, and there was great unemployment in both Canada and the United States, but the price of gold remained the same. So that made for a boom situation in Dawson. The town prospered in the 1930s. (Some of the big gold dredges were rebuilt in that period.) It made for tremendous traffic on the river, and a very prosperous situation in the Yukon, except for the fur traders. Freight and traffic for the lower river, which includes such places as Eagle, Fort Yukon, and Circle City in Alaska, had to be picked up in Dawson City, because there were no roads across from Fairbanks to those towns, like there are today. All that freight was brought down on the riverboats from Whitehorse to Dawson, and then reloaded onto the American steamboats, the *Yukon* and the *Alaska*. The NC shipped to those communities on the lower river.

Even most of the banking on the Alaskan side, was done through the Dawson NC. People would deposit their money with the company, and when they needed supplies they either charged, or paid for them with the money they had deposited. It made for a tremendous amount of bookkeeping because all those accounts had to be transferred to Seattle, which was the head office. It was a very busy time in the 1930s on the river.

There were a lot of big farms, that are still visible, above and below Dawson on the islands. There was also a government experimental farm, above Swede Creek. There was a tremendous amount of hay raised in the McQuesten Valley, back of Gravel Lake, and there was a road cut from that lake over to Dominion Creek. It came out at a creek that was called Utah. Many tons of hay came out of those valleys. One man had five or six huge greenhouses, where he raised beautiful tomatoes, cucumbers and radishes. There was an abundance of local potatoes around Dawson and the NC bought all they could locally. Tons of fresh whitefish were brought in from Ethel Lake, and sold at the store.

Chappie married his wife, Mattie, in 1934. They raised two children, a son, Bill, and a daughter, Betty, in Dawson City, where they went to school. (They continued their education in Mayo, when the family moved back there in 1951.) They lived in a big apartment over the store, which looked right out onto the river. Many times they saw great herds of caribou trying to cross the river, just above the town. "When I worked on the boats, I used to see large herds crossing the river. The boats would have to cut their motors and drift through them, in order not to harm any animals, but they paid no attention to the big ships at all. Just kept right on going until they all got across. And we used to see thousands of caribou on the 60 Mile road, (the one that goes up over the skyline, and then joins the Alaska Highway) but they're all gone now. You don't see any today."

Individuals were allowed to shoot two caribou a season, and most everyone went out and got their quota. The government in those days used to allow commercial hunting, and meat could be obtained that way. People relied heavily on the wild meat, and the local vegetables that were grown in Dawson, because the perishables that came from outside had to come up the coast from Vancouver to Skagway and the only refrigeration available was ice blocks, both on the White Pass railway, and the riverboats. In the hot weather the blocks wouldn't always hold out for the whole trip.

So the NC bought tons of caribou, sheep and moose meat from commercial hunters when hunting season was open and sold it in the store. "There was a cafe in Dawson then, called The Arcade Cafe," said Chappie, "It was in the old Royal Alexander Hotel right on front street. A man by the name of Harry Gleaves ran it. He put out special menus for the tourists, featuring moose, bear, sheep and caribou meat. Half the time, he would be out of everything except moose meat, so he would use various spices to flavor that meat—so each serving would be different. A group of tourists at the same table would sample each others sheep, or caribou, and compare it to the moose meat. 'You taste some of mine,' they would say. Most of them couldn't make up their mind which animal made the best meal, but decided they were all delicious eating. It was all moose-meat!"

The eggs, in particular, were hard to keep. They would be put into storage in the basement of the store, and sometimes kept until the first boat in the spring. By that time they had taken on quite a distinctive flavor. People got so used to eating the well-aged eggs that after awhile, when they went on a trip to Vancouver, and were offered fresh eggs...they wouldn't eat them, as they tasted flat.

There were a lot of egg stories circulating around Dawson, one of them being about a single miner, who was preparing his breakfast one morning, opened up a new carton of eggs, and found a written message on one of them, printed in tiny letters in ink. It said, "Would like to meet a rich miner. Matrimony in mind." And a Vancouver address was attached. The lonely miner thought a lot about that during the winter months in his cabin, and when spring came, he decided to take a trip south on the first steamboat of the season. Arriving in Seattle, he lost no time in making his way to Vancouver and finding the address of the egg lady. He showed up at her door in his brand new suit and tie, with great anticipation. A very pretty and pregnant young lady answered the door, and he explained why he had come.

"Well, you're a few years late," the lady said, "but if you've come that far, you'd might as well come in and meet my husband and two children." (I believe this was the theme of one of Robert Service's poems.)

The first boat in the spring was the big event of the season for the folks in Dawson City. In fact, even during school hours, the kids were allowed to go and watch the first arrival. The boat would blow three whistles at the mouth of the Klondike, just above town, and the kids would immediately depart from school. They wouldn't wait for the teacher to dismiss the class. She had no more authority, after that whistle blew.

Everyone in town would be on the wharf to see the people who had been away all winter. There would be oranges, apples and lots and lots of mail, including the all-important Eatons catalogue. And fresh eggs!

"Our son had his fifth birthday on one of the sternwheelers," Chappie said. "The chef did up a whole birthday party for him, cake and all." The service in the dining rooms on the river was superb; it matched the quality of the Princess boats on the coast. They had white linen tablecloths, silverware and dishes all embossed with the White Pass crest. You could have four meals a day if you wanted.

Whenever the boats stopped, some of the ladies and all the male passengers would get off and 'chew the rag,' and probably get in the way of the men that were trying to load the wood on the boats, but it made the trip more enjoyable for everyone. A few lucky passengers got a chance to visit the pilot house, and sometimes they were allowed to try their hand at the steering wheel, under the watchful eye of the captain...providing the boat was going upstream.

A person could sit there on the deck and listen to the paddlewheel beating the water; it made kind of a thrashing sound, the paddles seemed to hit the water. They put out a terrific spray, and the passengers would get on the back of the boat and watch them going around for hours. The engine crew, the stokers and deckhands, had sleeping cabins right in the engine room, right beside the big Pitman arms that were going back and forth all night. (Pitman arms were the two giant, power-driven wooden arms that held the paddlewheels, one on each side, and drove them around and around.) They would get used to the sound of the engines; it was a rhythmic sound and they slept like logs unless the motors stopped for some reason—then they would wake right up. The chief and second engineers had cabins on the top deck.

On the lower deck on the bow of the boat stood two tall spars, with a block and tackle attached to them. If a boat found itself grounded on a sandbar, a fairly common occurrence when the river was low, these spars would be used to help get off the bar. They would be lowered into the water, and the block and tackle hooked to the big steam winch, in the front of the boat. The cable would be taken up, and they could lift the front end of the boat in this manner. Then they'd tip the spars and this would jerk the boat along, and they could sort of walk it off the sandbar this way. Sometimes the problem arose when a boat came too close to a sandbar because the big paddle wheels sucked the water out from under the boat, leaving it dry so it would settle on the bar. When that happened, they would reverse the paddle wheels to throw water under the boat again, which would work sometimes, but not always, and that is when the spars would come into their own.

Carmacks was the largest community on the river in Chappie's time. There were a couple of stores there and a post office and a lot of freight was taken on and off the boats. "Our family traveled on the paddlewheelers quite a few times," he said. "And we liked going down on the coast boats. After you had been running that store all summer, and having people complaining about this and that—wanting credit and a hundred and one things—it was so good to just relax and spend four days going up the river to Whitehorse. All you did was play bridge, drink a beer once in a while, and listen to someone playing the piano. Or get off to visit some old-timer at a wood camp...it was a good life! Nowadays you go by airplane, and sit at the airport waiting for an hour sometimes, if the plane is late. Then, when you get to Edmonton, or Vancouver, it takes you an hour and a half to get into the city. Oh, it's faster, alright, but it's the rush I don't like. Everyone's in a hell of a rush! In the old steamboat days you got on a boat and you just relaxed the whole trip, going up the river."

When Chappie retired, the family moved to Whitehorse, which by then was the capital of the Yukon. "The moving of the capital to Whitehorse, and the closing down of the river traffic had quite a psychological effect on the people in Dawson City," he said. "It hurt to lose the title after all those years. But they survived, and the ones that did stay would probably never dream of living anywhere else."

Chappie made many trips on all the navigable rivers during his lifetime. He drifted down the Pelly once, right from Pelly Lakes to Fort Selkirk, in a boat with ribs made of willow bows, with a moose skin stretched over them. They got to Fort Selkirk, took their bags up to Taylor and Drury store, and when they went back to see if they had forgotten anything, they found that the dogs had eaten every bit of the boat except the ribs. He drifted down the Stewart with Mac Munroe and their two sons, for four glorious days, just drifting. "And I drifted down the Hootalinqua," he said, "and most of the way down the Yukon in a small boat."

The history that surrounds Dawson, is still very visible in places. It's a famous little town, and the tourism is getting greater every year. And who knows when someone will find another gold bonanza on a creek that the old-timers somehow missed. Back then when the cry of "Gold!" echoed back and forth in 'them thar hills,' thousands of people dropped whatever they were doing, and joined the great trek to the gold-fields of the Klondike.

7

The VanBibbers

This is the Law of the Yukon,
That only the Strong shall thrive;
That surely the Weak shall perish,
And only the Fit survive.

Robert Service

Ira VanBibber lived on the shore of the Pelly River, with his Indian wife 'Short' as he affectionately called her.

When we first met him he was just coming up from the river, where he had taken his daily swim. He was still in his swimming trunks, a towel thrown over his shoulder. He had an amazing physique for a man in his eighties; tall, muscular, and bronzed from the sun. We had just driven into his yard. We introduced ourselves, and he very cordially ushered us inside, calling to his wife who was in the kitchen: "Short!" he said, "We've got company. Bring out some of that home brew, will you?" We heard a loud pop and a minute or two later another one, followed by a hissing sound that reminded me of water gushing from a hose. Ira grinned, got up and motioned us to follow him. There in the kitchen was a round galvanized tub with two empty bottles standing in beer an inch deep on the bottom, and just as we entered the room Short popped the cap on a third. A geyser of the amber liquid shot out and once more she guided it into the tub, where the bottle quickly emptied. In exasperation, she thrust another one at Ira saying, "Here, you do it!"

"Now, Short," he laughed, "I told you the ones on that shelf were wild." And he reached into another cupboard and found some tamer brew. It was the start of a wonderful evening. He entertained us with fascinating tales of their past experiences.

Short's real name was Eliza. She was a Tlinget Indian of the Crow clan. There is no written record of her birth, but it is estimated to be in the early 1880s. Her mother, Alice, came from Juneau, and was one of Chief Jackson's five wives. Alice had run away, as one of the wives was jealous and had threatened to kill her. She joined a band that was heading for the Aishihik Lake area, and that was where her baby Eliza was born.

Eliza roamed about for years throughout the Yukon, Pelly and Stewart watersheds, following her mother, stepfather, stepbrothers and sisters, and eventually settling in Fort Selkirk, where she met this tall, soft-spoken man called Ira VanBibber. She decided right there that she would rather follow this man, from now on, and that's just what she did. "We've never had any regrets, either," said Ira, "but I have to tell you, old Short has worked in her lifetime. She dressed all fourteen of those kids...made their clothes out of moose skin when they were small, good clothes, too."

Ira was originally from West Virginia. He moved out West with the intention of becoming a cowboy, he told us. "But I kept falling off my horse." So he decided to try logging, instead. When the news of the gold rush hit the newspapers he and his brother, who was also a huge man (six-foot-seven in stature), teamed up to join the stampede. When they reached Skagway, they discovered that every man coming over the Pass, had to have a thousand pounds of supplies each, unless they were employed.

"Well, my brother and I didn't have the kind of dough it would take to buy all that," said Ira. "We thought we might have to turn back. But then we met a fellow there, that they called Whiskey Jack, who was looking for someone to help him pack $50,000 worth of liquor over the trail." Apparently Jack had noticed these two strong-looking men, and figured they were just what he was looking for. He hired them on the spot, the job became their ticket to the Klondike.

A year or two later, Ira was hauling mail by dog team from Dawson City to Whitehorse over the Yukon River. Next, he prospected and trapped in the Selkirk area, where he met Eliza in the early 1900s.

Ira told us the tale of their long trek with their baby, Leta, in 1908. They traveled on foot to the headwaters of the Pelly and Ross rivers. Eliza's cousin Tommy Joe went with them. He was only fourteen years old then, but was a good help in the bush. There were no roads—or even trails—in that country then. They went up over the rugged Mackenzie mountains and on to the head of the South Nahanni (the 'Headless Valley'). Their route took them over sheer peaks, through swamps and bogs, and buckbrush for miles and miles. It took them about a year to make the trip.

It was certainly incredible to think of any woman, least of all a pregnant one, being along on a trip like that! But somewhere on that wild and rough terrain their second baby, May, was born.

They trapped and prospected there on the Nahanni, close to the breathtakingly beautiful Virginia Falls (which is actually higher than the famous Niagara Falls) until 1911, when they returned to the Pelly.

Ira went into the game guiding business, and built a huge two-story log home at Mica Creek on the banks of the Pelly river—the very same home we were sitting in now, many years later...listening enthralled as his words painted pictures of their life and adventures.

Ira and Short had sixteen children all told, two of them died as babies, and fourteen are well-known and respected Yukon citizens.

One of them, Alex, grew up to be quite a famous big game guide and outfitter working from his home in the village of Champagne. He gave us the following account of what his early childhood, at Christmas time in particular, was like.

"When we kids were little, the family moved around between the mouth of the Pelly, Fort Selkirk, Ross River, and up the MacMillan. I got my first schooling at Fort Selkirk, from old Mrs. Cowaret. She was the mission lady there, and she taught some of us kids for a while. She used those old slate boards to teach us arithmetic. From there we went to a boarding school in Dawson, and to the public school from there.

"To get to school in Dawson, in September, we used a raft. My dad couldn't see us paying for tickets on a sternwheeler when the river ran in that direction, anyway. So he built a raft, and loaded us on it with a bunch of vegetables. Before he pushed us out into the current, the old man would give us some advice. 'If the raft starts to get water-logged, just pull into a drift pile and tie a few more logs on, to give it some buoyancy. It'll keep floating that way.' We were still pretty young, and scared of bears, so most of the time we would sleep right on the raft. When we did spend the night on the beach, we'd make sure we were real close to that raft, and if we heard any noises we didn't waste any time poling it out into the river again. All us kids would just huddle together in an old broken down sleeping bag, that we'd sell, or just throw away, after we got to the other end.

"My dad used to run his large family like a company project. He could only afford to send four of us to school at once. As a child got to be school age, he had to pull the oldest out, so he or she could help with the trapping—or something else around the place—to help support the others. So none of us got too much schooling. He was paying what was then the large sum of $25 per month, per child, to stay in this hostel, which belonged to a church organization. There were thirty or forty other kids there besides us, mostly all mixed-race kids.

"When Christmas came along we had a real celebration. We decorated a big community tree, and hung up our socks, which they'd fill with candy, and little gifts. Then in the evening we got to see both Mr. and Mrs. Santa Claus. It was the first time I'd ever heard of Mrs. Santa Claus, but there she was, dressed just like Santa himself. They jumped around with a

Ho, ho, ho! and gave out presents, and we thought they were both for real.

"After our schooling was over, we came back home, and went out on the trapline. Christmas from then on was strictly a family affair. Just a couple of days set aside to rest, and be all together. We were usually scattered all over the mountains, on our trapline, which was about 100 miles square. Game and fur was plentiful, and we were happy there. A family raised in the bush, just surviving. The girls in the family trapped and worked just as hard as the boys did. We didn't worry about registering, or game laws or anything in those days. It was just a matter of survival. Mother and dad trapped right around the base camp, and the rest of us kids strung out with our dog teams, but we always managed to get back and spend Christmas together.

"We'd bring in some fat sheep meat, or young moose and just feast and rest for a few days. We were too far from the stores to buy candy, and treats like that, but we made up little gifts for each other. And sometimes we'd send for some records or small gifts from the Eatons catalogue, and exchange them at Christmas time. We had one of those crank gramophones that you'd crank up and play. Before we ever started school, we had a cylinder-type record player that played tube records. I wish I'd saved that, it would be something to own today.

"When we were older, starting in the 1940s, we spent our Christmas at Champagne, and they had a real hoe-down, with fiddle music and everything. At that time the trading post was in full swing at Champagne. All the boys would come in and sell their furs, and they'd have money in their pockets to buy fancy groceries, and turkeys and the odd bottle of wine. That was still in the days of the home-brew making. They would celebrate and dance steady. The all-night dances would last sometimes for a week.

"It was an entirely different atmosphere in those days at Christmas time. They really knew how to do it up right!"

II

The Paddlewheelers

8

James Moran

—•◆•—

Wild and wide are my borders,
Stern as death is my sway;
From my ruthless throne
I have ruled alone,
For a million years and a day.

Robert Service

It was in the middle of June, and the water was very, very swift when the first *Klondike* was wrecked, just past the 30 Mile River. It hit a rock, which put it out of commission as far as the steering was concerned. The motors were no longer effective, and the *Klondike* struggled downstream for three or four miles, finally settling down on a sandbar.

"There was many people from down south who were pulling up stakes and heading to the Yukon, on spec, in those days," said Jimmy Moran, who was working on the boat at the time. "It was because of the depression." There were quite a few passengers on board. Some were families with children, going to different wood camps, or to the mines at Dawson and Mayo. A lot of their furniture and most of their belongings were lost on that trip. Some were single men just looking for work.

"One of the crew members on the steamboat this day was a fellow by the name of Malcolm McLeod, who had worked as first mate on the river (mainly on the *Klondike*) for about twenty years. He was a well-respected, capable man and that day was the first time he had ever taken over the wheel. Usually the captain, or the skipper, would be at the wheel; it was customary to take six hours each. But at certain times, different members of the crew were allowed to take over, especially when they were in an easy stretch of the river."

In 1978, Jimmy Moran still remembered that day forty-two years earlier, the day of the boat wreck. "Because of the large influx of passengers, I got a temporary promotion," he said, "From mess boy to waiter. I was waiting table in the dining room of the *Klondike*, when all of a sudden the old girl hit a rock. From then on we were helpless as far as the current was concerned. A big shudder shook the ship—then everything went—the tables slid along, the chairs fell over, and everything slid off the tray.

"At that particular time, I was looking after the officer's table. Captain Coghlin, had taken an extra-long shift, because of having a new skipper at the wheel (Malcolm). He had stayed with him all through the rough water at 30 Mile so he had slept late, and was just having breakfast now. He always had the same thing: oatmeal and prunes. I just got through serving him when the big jolt came, and the "Old Man" (an endearing term for Captain Coghlin) just jumped up and headed for the wheelhouse. Almost everybody else went out onto the afterdeck where there was lots of room, to see what had happened."

They could see slivers of the boat in the water, for one thing. Captain Coghlin was in the wheelhouse by now, and they could see him spinning the wheel, but nothing was happening. The steering gear had gone with that first jolt, and the engines had been crippled. The boat was at the mercy of the current.

There were many women and children on board, and it was amazing how they kept their calm. The lifeboats were lowered, and the passengers got in. There were two expert oarsmen, Red Halcott and a fellow by the name of Hamilton. They rowed to the closest shore, which happened to be an island, which was later named Mosquito Island, because they just about ate those people alive. The men who were rowing didn't have nearly as much work as the women who were baling like mad—because those boats were dried right out, and leaking badly.

"I remember watching them," Jimmy Moran said. "That lifeboat was full of women and children, and just as it nudged the shore of that island, it sank, and they all scrambled out."

There were many bends in the river, and the boat kept drifting from side to side, hitting land and changing its direction each time. And every time it hit, some deckhands would jump out and make an effort to get a cable on her and around a tree, but they weren't able to do it quickly enough. The boat would bounce out into midstream again, and next time it hit a bend they would try again. Some of the fellows stayed where they were on the shore, after their unsuccessful try to tie the boat up. All this time, it was slowly sinking, and eventually the crew was advised that everyone who could get off had better do it now. There were crew members scattered all along the river bank for three and a half miles. The boat sank until only the wheelhouse and part of the upper deck was visible. It came up again one more time, before hitting the sandbar, where it remained.

One of the deckhands on the *Klondike*, Andy Kaye, got caught out on the bow, as she was going down, and couldn't get off. He was lucky enough to just catch a gangplank that was floating along in the water. He jumped on this, and floated for several miles along the river. A boat picked him up there on the bank, later in the day.

Walter Israel managed to scramble up onto the wheelhouse, and rode her through to the final sandbank.

While the crippled boat was drifting along, the cargo had been gradually floating out and downriver. Those Indians and settlers along the next stretch of river found furniture and supplies they had never seen before. And because of all the sacks of flour that they were able to salvage, many had free bread for months. They also snagged cardboard cartons of cigarettes out of the river, which were very well sealed, and remained in perfect condition.

As soon as it was obvious to the crew that the boat was going to go down, they had cut the ropes on the three horses and one cow, so they would at least have a chance to survive. The horses all swam safely to shore, but the cow didn't make it. She was the only casualty of the disaster. Incredibly, there were no injuries in that whole crew of twenty-seven men, and fifty-two passengers.

All along the river was a telegraph line, from Whitehorse to Dawson City and beyond. The telegraph operators had offices every twenty miles along the whole route. A purser on the boats could tap into that line with his equipment, so it wasn't too long until a motor boat came along (that would be the fuelage that Pauline LePage referred to in her story) and picked everyone up. They all congregated on a small island, not too far from where the ship sank, and set up camp. They were able to salvage some groceries off the boat, because the galley on the *Klondike* was on the upper deck, and they found blankets and pillows, so they were comfortable there for the time being.

Gradually, some of the group was picked up by other boats, and most of the crew were flown back by small plane to Whitehorse. Within thirty-six hours everyone was back where they belonged. Without most of their belongings, unfortunately.

The riverboats carried passengers, almost all tourists, from every state in the Union, all over Canada, and some even came from Europe. The SS *Casca* carried up to ninety passengers, and had a crew of around twenty-five.

In 1936, Dr. Jimmy Moran, who was working his way through dental college, took on the job of mess boy, which paid $70 per month. He peeled all the potatoes and vegetables, cleaned up the crew's mess, washed dishes and pots and pans. Waiters got $60, a demotion really, as far as wages were concerned, but the tips made up for the difference, and the job was a lot easier. The pantryman could earn as much as $85 a month, which was very good money at that time. He acted as a go-between for the chef, the cooking staff, and the waiters. He had to do all the carving, and stack the dumb-waiter. (Most of the boats had these dumb-waiters, but not the *Klondike 1.*

The dumb waiter was like a small elevator, or lift, that sent food and dishes up and down, from kitchen to dining room.) The pantryman had to make all the salads, and he would also be responsible for the table centerpieces.

All wages on the boats were found (meaning they included room and board), and they included the fare up from Vancouver in the spring and back again in the fall.

Many of the crew had little sidelines going, as a means of supplementing their salaries. The deck hands helped to load ore, for which they got extra pay. The pantryman would get a percentage of the tips from the waiters for helping out when they were exceptionally busy. The chef sold day-old bread and baking to people at the wood camps, and the mess boy sold all the food scraps he could save to Indians and wood cutters, for their dogs.

(Author's note: My brother Ray had the job of mess boy on one of the steamers, when he was in his teens. The skipper on that boat used to take it on himself to sell the scraps when they made a 'wood stop.' The mess boy would have to save it all for him in a big bucket that was kept on the lower deck.

The weather had been extremely hot for a couple of days and these scraps were getting pretty high. "You could have smelled them a mile away," Ray said. He finally got fed up with this, "I'm going to throw it overboard," he thought. He looked all around to make sure nobody was close by, then, being a fairly strong fellow, he picked up the pail by the handle and gave it a mighty swing over his head. Just as he was going to let go of the handle, he heard the skipper's voice right behind him. "HOLD IT!" Instinctively his fingers tightened around the handle of the pail which was in midair—and the momentum of all the weight pulled him right over the edge of the boat and into the river. The crew quickly threw him a lifeline, and a very bedraggled young man was hauled back up on the boat, with lettuce leaves clinging to his hair.)

The only refrigeration they had on the boat, were blocks of ice, taken on at Whitehorse. Each boat had several ice boxes, and a meat cooler, or 'meat-house,' as they were called. The lack of sufficient refrigeration was one of the main con-

The SS *Prospector* taking on cordwood along the Stewart River. Note the woodpile on the bank, the lower deck piled with wood and the passengers on the upper deck. Sometime after 1901.　　　*Yukon Archives: Goetzman photo, Bassoc Collection (UAA)*

Two men poling up the river near Whitehorse in an open boat named *Boston*.

River travel: three men pulling a boat up the White River.

Two men unloading sacks of mail from their canoe after transporting it across the Yukon River before freeze up. *Yukon Archives: MLB Collection*

The wreck of the SS *Klondike* sunk in the Yukon River below Hootalinqua. June, 1936. *Yukon Archive: C. Tidd Collection*

The ravages of spring breakup can be seen in this view of the Yukon Crossing Roadhouse and Stable, near Rink Rapids on the Yukon River.

Yukon Archives: Harbottle Collection

Claude Tidd approaches the Tidd's cabin at Twelve Mile (in the Dawson area) carrying snowshoes. 1938-39. *Yukon Archives: C. Tidd Collection*

Thomas Tugwell standing next to a horse that is hitched to pull timber logs at Log Cabin, B.C. The Log Cabin Hotel is visible in the background.

Yukon Archives: AHS Collection

A view of the Shaeffer's roadhouse on Mica Creek near Pelly Crossing. The Shaeffers and Dave Fotheringham pose at the front door of their roadhouse. 1924-25.

Yukon Archives: Hare Collection

Betty Taylor, Charlie Taylor's wife, interrupts a dog sled trip to pose with her dog, Timber (left), and Charlie's dog, Fiscal. 1930s.

Yukon Archives: Charles D. Taylor Collection

A man loading furs onto a dog sled in front of the Taylor and Drury Post at Ross River. March, 1928.

Yukon Archives: C. Tidd Collection

Charlie Taylor's snowmobile or half-track in front of the old Regina Hotel. The half-track was made from two Chevrolet cars. 1930s.

Yukon Archives: Charles D. Taylor Collection

Claude Tidd and three other men standing around a Caterpillar tractor and a dog team outside the roadhouse at Carmacks. 1924. *Yukon Archives: C. Tidd Collection*

Four men and their canoe resting on an ice floe floating on the Yukon River. 1899.

Yukon Archives: E. A. Hegg Collection (UW)

The Taylor and Drury supply boat *Thistle*, newly bought, on Teslin Lake. 1919.

Yukon Archives: L. Irvine Collection

SS *Yukoner* going through Five Finger Rapids. Passengers and crew are on deck. 1900-02. *Yukon Archives: E. J. Hamacher and J. Doody photo, MM Collection*

Men loading the Canadian Bank of Commerce gold shipment onto a sternwheeler in Dawson. 1899. *Yukon Archives: Larss and Duclos photo, Roozeboom Collection*

A card party in progress, while the SS *Rock Island* steams its way to Dawson. Far right seated at the table are W. H. Stevens and R. P. McLennan. 1898.

Yukon Archives: McLennan Collection

Bow shot of sternwheeler *Clifford Sifton* steaming through turbulent Miles Canyon, with three sweeps extended over the bow. July 24, 1900.

Yukon Archives: H. C. Barley photo, Pinneo Collection (UAA)

A large crowd assembled to watch the last spike being driven at Bennett. There are three sternwheelers at anchor on the the lake: *Australian, Gleaner* and *Clifford Sifton.* July 6, 1899.   *Yukon Archives: E. A. Hegg Collection*

Some members of the Northwest Mounted Police talking outside log buildings at the Tagish post. 1898 *Yukon Archives: MM Collection*

The Taylor and Drury store at Carmacks, with people posing on the boardwalk. Advertising signs are visible on the storefront. 1913. *Yukon Archives: Cecil Swanson Collection*

The VanBibbers standing in front of a group of cabins: Ira VanBibber, in the center, Eliza VanBibber, woman holding baby, and ten of their children. 1930s.

Yukon Archives: May Menzies Collection

Ira and Eliza VanBibber outside their home at Pelly Crossing.

Chuck Beaumont.

Beaumont Collection

The SS *Whitehorse* docked at a wood camp along the Yukon River. Note the passengers and crew on the deck.   *Yukon Archives: Read photo, MM Collection*

A view of the sternwheeler *Keno* pushing a barge loaded with ore sacks, machinery and fuel drums just off the river bank in Mayo. 1940s.   *Yukon Archives: Hare Collection*

The police and mail delivery dog teams in front of the government telegraph office in Carcross (later to become the Carcross Post Office). Down the street, a number of buildings and a sternwheeler are visible. 1922.   *Yukon Archives: C. Tidd Collection*

A Klondike Airways freight crew—Bud Harbottle (back to camera), Louis Irvine (facing camera) and Neil Keobke (holding box)—unloading crates of turkeys, quarters of beef and mail from a truck to transfer to a sled, then to a canoe, in order to cross the unfrozen section of the river. 1936.   *Yukon Archives: L. Irvine Collection*

Andrew Cruikshank with a long string of dogs near the steep bank of a river. 1920-30s.
Yukon Archives: C. Tidd Collection

Claude Tidd having a cup of tea at a winter camp. April, 1939.
Yukon Archives: C. Tidd Collection

A string of dog teams and their Indian owners posing by a cabin on their return from a caribou hunt in the northern Yukon. 1921.

A Klondike Airways crew camping on the north side of the river. From left to right are Frank Slim, T. C. Richards and Carl Chambers. April, 1936.

The Klondike Airways mail launch—a tunnel boat powered by a Model A marine conversion engine—docked in front of the telegraph station at Carmacks. Benny Evans on the left, Louis Irvine on the right. 1936. *Yukon Archives: L. Irvine Collection*

Bow shot of SS *Sarah* docked at Dawson in a river front scene. 1900.

A view of the Yukon Gold Company's buildings of Guggieville, almost totally surrounded by dredge tailings. Canadian Klondike Mining Company dredge Canadian No. 4 is seen working on the bottom right. 1915-22.

A miner pushing an ore cart along the rails into a tunnel at the Venus Mine in the Conrad area. 1906.

These passengers are disembarking from the Taku Tram, a small train that ran between Atlin Lake and Taku Landing, and boarding the sternwheeler *Tutshi*. Late 1920s. *Yukon Archives: M. Taylor photo, Jean Campbell Collection*

Two men maneuver a raft of logs down the Yukon River with long oars. 1920s. *Yukon Archives: C. Tidd Collection*

Two large, flat-bottom barges with sweeps lashed together and loaded with freight and passengers. The barges were owned by Messereau and Clark Scows. May, 1905.

Yukon Archives: J. Doody photo, MLB Collection

Four men on a loaded barge with sweeps at either end in the ice at Dawson: the last arrival of the season. October 27, 1900.   *Yukon Archives: MM Collection*

A long range panorama of Whitehorse looking toward the southwest from across the river. Numerous sternwheelers are docked at wharves and steaming on the river. 1901.

Yukon Archives: Vancouver Public Library Collection

A crew member of the sternwheeler *Yukon* feeds a piece of wood from a wood camp into the boiler. June, 1932. *Yukon Archives: C. Tidd Collection*

The *Alaska* being launched from timber skids in Whitehorse Shipyards dry dock. The *Bonanza King* is partially visible in the background. 1915. *Yukon Archives: MM Collection*

The Takhini River crossing on the old Dawson road. A rope-pulled barge is crossing with two vintage automobiles laden with supplies. Log buildings from the old settlement are on the far shore. 1920. *Yukon Archives: Harbottle Collection*

A Klondike Airways freight and mail truck and driver, Fred Boss, that have broken through the ice on the Takhini River. 1937. *Yukon Archives: L. Irvine Collection*

A partial panorama of the cabins and buildings of Carcross. A docked sternwheeler and the railroad swing bridge are visible. 1900.

Yukon Archives: J. Doody photo, MM Collection

Two men, sitting on a wagon filled with hay, rest their horses on Second Avenue in Dawson. A tailor shop, a laundromat, the K. C. Short Order House and an elevated board sidewalk are visible. 1901. *Yukon Archives: Adams, Larkin and Cantwell Collection*

A team of horses is pulling a small cart with driver along the railroad tracks at Taku. The Taku Hotel and other log buildings are in the background. 1898.

Yukon Archives: E. A. Hegg Collection (UW)

A stern view of the *Tutshi* docked at Engineer Mines along the shore of the Taku Arm. The dock facility, a number of buildings and a few small boats are all visible. 1920s.

Yukon Archives: L. C. Read photo, AHS Collection

The *Queen of the Yukon* G-CAHR being towed by a team of horses, belonging to Archibald Close, down the frozen Stewart River to Mayo after the engine quit. November, 1927.   *Yukon Archives: Harbottle Collection*

A Ryan B-1 monoplane, sister ship to the *Spirit of St. Louis*, owned by Yukon Airways and Exploration Co. This shot was taken in Skagway, Alaska, with (from left to right) J. E. Smith, engineer; W. A. (Bill) Monday; Lt. A. D. Cruikshank; and Clyde G. Wann. 1927.   *Yukon Archives: Harbottle Collection*

The *Claire* and pilot Everett Wasson. 1930. *Yukon Archives: Wood Collection*

A woman standing on the upper deck of the sternwheeler *Whitehorse* on the Dawson run as it passes sternwheelers up on skids at Lower Laberge.

Yukon Archives: MLB Collection

cerns of the chef. Most of the meat came from Vancouver. The beef, pork, lamb and bacon was all frozen, when it was put on the boats. They picked it up from the cold storage in Whitehorse. The White Pass maintained a huge commissary there, for the purpose of storing food supplies, when they arrived from Skagway by train. They would be held there until they were loaded onto the steamboats.

One of the main chores of the galley staff was to keep the meat in as good a condition as possible, until it was all used. They would trim it, wipe it regularly with cheesecloth soaked in vinegar, and keep it fairly palatable for the duration of the trip.

In those days, it was legal to sell moose and caribou, and the boats would occasionally take on a quarter of meat, bought from Indians in the area; the transaction negotiated by the chief steward, to augment their fresh meat supply. The passengers really enjoyed the wild meat. The most popular dish though, was the fresh, succulent lake trout, and whitefish. They had an abundance of that delicacy all season long. Most of it was supplied by an Indian chief, by the name of Jim Boss, who lived and fished at Lake Laberge.

The red spring, or "king" salmon came up from the coast to spawn, and they had ample supply of these. These fish arrived at Dawson in very good shape, having made a comparatively easy and short trip to their spawning grounds. Some of them weighed fifty and sixty pounds each.

The long summer days in the north country (almost twenty-four hours of daylight in June) produced some excellent vegetable gardens along the river and at Dawson City. The paddlewheelers were fortunate to be able to purchase plenty of local salad greens, lettuce, tomatoes, radishes, cucumbers and green onions, which were of wonderful quality. So the cuisine in the dining room was greatly enjoyed and appreciated, by both passengers and crew.

The huge paddlewheelers drew very little water, being flat-bottomed, and they could pull up almost anywhere along the banks of the river, provided there were no sandbars to obstruct them. The wood for firing up the steam boilers was of supreme importance, as the ships could not run without it. They burned an average of a cord an hour, and wood camps flourished along the river.

The cutters worked year-round at this job. Many of them had built decent cabins and had their wives and children with them.

One of the functions of the riverboats was to stop wherever anyone left a white flag on the bank close to their camp. Sometimes the woodcutter or fox rancher would be nowhere in sight, but he would leave money in an envelope, with a list of items he needed. And quite often he would request that his change would be brought back in postage stamps. Someone on the boat would take on the responsibility of filling the order to the best of their ability.

Merrit Island was one of Happy LePage's wood camps. Walter Israel came to the Yukon, from Mt. Lehman, British Columbia, about this time; the boat dropped him off at Happy's camp, and he never looked back. He loved the life and the country, and stayed to eventually become a very prominent business man in Carmacks.

Mrs. Catherine Mulloy was one of the finest shots in the Yukon, and a very colorful character to boot. All the old-timers in the Yukon still talk about the time the SS *Casca* was making her last voyage of the season. She was heading north upstream to Whitehorse, and Captain Morrison never noticed the white flag that Mrs. Mulloy had left along the shore. He was sailing merrily along in the middle of the river, and had almost got by Mulloy's camp, when a blast from her double-barrelled shotgun went off and the flag on the wheelhouse, just above his ear, went flying into the river. It didn't take Captain Morrison long to ease over and stop along the bank to pick up the potatoes that she was shipping off to the market in Whitehorse. Mrs. Mulloy made very sure they weren't going to miss the last boat of the season.

Most of the time she would be seen in her in her old jeans and cowboy hat with a gun in her hands, but whenever she made a trip to town on one of the boats she traveled in style, all dressed in silk or satin, and wearing lace gloves. She could be tough and rough, and out-swear any of the miners in the area...or she could be a very elegant, well-bred lady when she so chose. Mrs. Mulloy was an expert trapper, and had furs nailed all over their cabin. She worked just like a man. Everyone wondered if her husband ever did anything to help.

Any time someone wanted to move camps, equipment or cattle to a new spot on the river, the White Pass boats would stop by, pick up the outfit, and take it to the new location.

From Whitehorse, and all across Lake Laberge, right to the 30 Mile River there was nothing but crystal-clear water. The best water in the world...pollution was unheard of there. The boats would collect enough of that clear water in barrels, to last until they got back again, because as the river gradually widened out and wound its way through mud flats on the way to Stewart the water just got muddier. Each tributary coming into the Yukon added to the silt, first the Hootalinqua, then Big Salmon, the Little Salmon, and the White River (which came by its name because of the silt deposits constantly piling up at the river's mouth which caused the water to actually look opaque). The silt got into the boilers and the boats would have to regularly tie up at Dawson for a day to clean them out.

Dr. Moran finished his training as a dentist after his riverboat days were over, and set up practice near his home town of Mt. Lehman, British Columbia.

9

Chuck Beaumont's Story

There's a land where the mountains are nameless,
And the rivers all run God knows where,
There are lives that are erring and aimless,
And deaths that just hang by a hair;
There are hardships that nobody reckons;
There are valleys unpeopled and still;
There's a land—oh it beckons and beckons,
And I want to go back—and I will.

Robert Service

Chuck Beaumont left Vancouver to go to work for White Pass as a deckhand in 1932, when he was nineteen years old. He worked there until his retirement in January, 1978. He had put in forty-six years with the same company.

Most of the boat crews had to be hired outside of the Yukon, because there just weren't the young men available for work. They recruited them from various towns in lower B.C. For most of the men, experience wasn't necessary. Chuck said jokingly, "A deckhand just had to have a strong back and flat feet. I didn't know what I was getting into, when I first went up there. I was as green as grass, and had never turned a wheel in my life. The first couple of trips, when I was decking on the *Keno*, I didn't know if I'd survive or not. But once you get into the swing of things, and those muscles get hardened up,

132

there's no better life. You get good food, good air, adequate amount of sleep if you needed it, and lots of exercise. The deckhands had to load all the wood onto the boats at the wood camps. They used little two-wheel trucks, which they wheeled onto a ramp built out of gangplanks. They loaded as much as fifteen cords onto the boat in forty minutes, which was the record, I believe."

The *Keno* in those days was assigned to the Stewart River service, a 180-mile run from the confluence of the Stewart and Yukon rivers to Mayo.

In those days they were still shipping silver ore from the Keno Hill Mining Company, and they shipped barge loads of the concentrates from Mayo, and deposited them in sacks, on the shore of Stewart City at the mouth of the Stewart. There were tons and tons of these sacks stockpiled on the bank in a single layer. They were continuously picked up and loaded onto the main riverboats, which would be coming back from Dawson. They stopped with their big barges on the way upstream to Whitehorse. From there the ore was shipped to Vancouver or Tacoma, or Bradley, Idaho.

The *Keno* very seldom got into Dawson City, and when it did it was a big event for the crew. They would go down there to wash the boilers, and in the odd emergency if someone was sick. The fellows on the boat would get pretty bored with this run. In Dawson, they could kick up their heels and enjoy the gambling and night life.

Chuck was on the *Keno* for five years, as deckhand and purser, and was then transferred to the main tourist boat. The *Casca* was the biggest steamboat on the river in those days, and operated on the Yukon River on a once-a-week round-trip schedule.

The American tourists came from Whitehorse to Dawson, and then connected with the steamer *Yukon*, went down the lower river to Nenana (which is on the Alaska side), took the Alaska railroad back to Seward, and sailed back to Seattle from there.

The year 1936 was a bad one for the White Pass. It lost two steamboats, the *Klondike* and the *Casca*, within thirty days of each other. It's not too often a company can survive a tragedy such as that, but the White Pass managed to. The *Klondike* sank first, then the *Casca* hit the submerged hulk of the old SS *Dawson* which had gone down in the Rink Rapids in 1926. This tore a great gaping wound in the bow of the vessel, and the water just flowed in.

Chuck had the job of going ashore with the pilot to notify the company that they wouldn't be bringing the boat back that week. The pilot was the famous Kid Marion. He said, "Don't worry, Chuck, I'll talk to the boss. You won't have to worry."

They took along the old portable radio phone, which Chuck always described as being "bigger than a breadbox, but smaller than a barn," carried it into the bush, and hooked a long rod with a metal tip on the end over the old iron telegraph line. They had to create a ground by stamping a big, preferably wet, spike into the ground. Then they cranked the handle, and this way they could reach the closest operator who would relay the message on to Whitehorse.

"Eventually," said Chuck, "we were able to get hold of Mr. Gordon, who was the superintendant of the river division. Marion said, 'Mr. Gordon, this is Kid Marion.'"

"Yes," came the answer, "what's on your mind?"

"Just a minute, the purser here wants to speak to you," and with those words, Kid handed the phone over to Chuck, with a wicked grin. Mr. Gordon listened to the bad news.

"There was a dull, sickening thud at the other end of the line, and I didn't know whether the boss fell down, or the phone dropped out of his hand, or what," said Chuck.

The boat had settled in water about four or five feet above the freight deck. "So all the deckhands and the galley people and the engineers had to scurry like hell to get up the ladders to the passenger deck."

All the passengers were in the dining room, when disaster struck. They heard a crunch and went outside to see what had happened. "When they saw the boat heading the wrong way, and starting to settle lower in the water, they knew she'd really 'come a cropper,'" said Chuck.

They took the people by lifeboat, with some of the deckhands and a cook, down to Yukon Crossing to the old winter roadhouse. It had been closed for the summer, but they set up a temporary camp there for the passengers until they could be picked up. They were able to get all the supplies and food they wanted from the *Casca*. That evening some planes arrived from Dawson, and picked up the passengers. They arrived at their destination much quicker than if they had finished the journey on the boat.

Among the passengers on the boat were five Anglican ministers, going to Dawson City to attend a synod there. Kid Marion said, "No wonder the ship went down with all that power on board."

A young couple by the name of Adami had a wood camp on the river at Williams Creek. They hadn't been married very long and a few months earlier they had ordered a whole outfit of furniture for their home, including a stove, which was all sent up on the *Klondike*. And of course, unfortunately, it had all gone down on the *Klondike* when that boat sank. "Well," they thought, "we had a good winter last year, and no one ever said that life would be easy on the river." So they ordered up another batch. Guess what boat that came up on. The *Casca*! And then it had gone down, too. They did manage to salvage some pieces, but a lot of it was never found. They began to wonder whether their life in the Yukon was going to be worth it or not!

The rest of the crew rode the crippled boat to her resting place, two or three miles down the river. Then they went up to the roadhouse and stayed there for a couple of days.

They were able to save all the mail, and most of the luggage, luckily, because it was all piled on a layer of 200 gallon oil drums, which lined the whole freight deck. The drums were four-feet tall and weighed about 1000 pounds each. So the mail was still high and dry when the boat grounded.

Little by little, though, as the water seeped through the boat, it settled deeper into the sand, the rest of the cargo from the vessel started floating downsteam.

"I remember one of the stewards saying, 'Hey, let's have some cantaloupe for breakfast.' And he went down and har-

135

pooned a crate of cantaloupe as it floated by. We lived very high off the hog for a few days there."

The crew from the *Casca* was transferred to the steamer *Nasutlin* to finish out the season, and in the fall a group of men from the shipyards, including Alec Mackintosh, the foreman, was sent down from Whitehorse to the wreck, where they salvaged the boiler, paddlewheel, engines, the Pitman arms, and anything usable that they could from the *Casca*.

As purser on the boat, Chuck had to obtain signatures for all the freight that was delivered along the river and he collected the money for whatever was not prepaid. So he got to know a lot of people and was always impressed by their honesty. One day the boat stopped at Kirkman Creek, a white flag had been put out at the mailbox on the bank. He collected the letters, and found one addressed to the purser. "Will you take this gold poke to the bank in Dawson?" It was a long poke, about eight-inches long, and two inches in diameter, made out of moosehide. "You could feel it was solid chunks of gold," said Chuck. "Well, of course, all the tourists were standing on deck, looking down and watching all this going on. When I came aboard again, they crowded around and one of them asked what was in the bag. Oh, I told him, I just picked up a poke of gold to take to the bank in Dawson. 'Don't believe it.' said the man. So I told him, 'Well here—heft this thing,' and I gave it to him and it just dropped out of his hand, because the gold is so heavy, you know."

"'Do you mean to tell me someone just left that thing sitting in the mailbox?' the man asked in amazement. 'Yeah, they trust me to take it down there,'" said Chuck.

"But what if someone else picked it up instead?" the man insisted. He could not believe that anyone could be that trusting.

Schooling was always a bit of a problem for families on the river. If they could afford it, some of them would board their children in town for the school season. In the more remote areas where they couldn't do this, the mothers had to give the children correspondence lessons. They would get a month's worth of lessons at a time by mail—and send them back out the same way. This worked until they got to high school age, and then it was a matter of having to send them to town. Raising children along the river, especially in the winter time, did present certain problems, but it was a healthy life. The snow was very clean, and the kids would come in from playing and shake themselves off, and they'd be bone dry. "Out here," said Chuck, "they go out and in ten minutes they're sopping wet. The folks who could afford to, sent their kids outside to school, but the ones who couldn't just had to make the best of it."

There was a telegraph operator at Stewart, at one point, who used to move across the river, where the line was, and live there in the summer. When the boats were running and there were more people around, he couldn't stand it, because it was too crowded for him. He liked his solitude. People like that didn't mind the winters, they just sort of hibernated.

"The Eatons catalogue was a best seller," Chuck joked, "but really, the 'Book of the Month' was quite popular up there. I remember Bill Hayes, who was a telegraph operator at Carmacks, subscribed to it. He was a very well-read and educated man. At Selwyn, there was a lady by the name of Mrs. Detraz. She had been a dance hall girl in Dawson many years earlier, and moved to Selwyn with her husband, who later died there. Mrs. Detraz was well thought of along the river, even though she had a voice like a bullhorn," Chuck said.

She was a big energetic woman with a keen sense of humor. They used to pick her up and take her to Dawson occasionally, on the steamer. One of these trips happened to fall on her birthday. Chuck told the steward this, and it was decided to bake her a cake.

When Kid Marion heard about it he said, "Let's fix Ma Detraz; we'll bake her a cake too, but it won't be made out of cake! It'll be a very special one." They went down and cut the end off a piece of cordwood, about twelve inches in diameter, and four inches thick. Then they smoothed it off a bit, and had the baker put icing all over it.

In the dining room that night, Mrs. Detraz was seated at the head of the captain's table, which they had tastefully set with a fresh wild flower arrangement, and the waiters sang "Happy Birthday to You." Then it was time for her to blow out the candles and cut the cake. She had a big knife, and three times she tried to get that knife blade into the cake. The fourth try she stabbed it as hard as she could, then she put the knife down and looked across the table to where the captain was sitting, trying real hard to keep his face in order. She stood up and hollered at the top of her voice, "Marion, you son-of-a-bitch, you jobbed me!" Chuck said he thought the tourists that were sitting around the dining room would fall out of their chairs from laughing. Then the real cake was brought in, and the party continued.

The river people got to know the boat crews better than they did their neighbors, because they saw them a lot more often. "In a way," Chuck said, "the river, from Whitehorse to Dawson City, was like one big community—450 miles long, with the neighbors living forty miles apart. They didn't get to visit each other very often, but the telegraph line could be accessed almost anywhere along the river, and news traveled fairly quickly if it was important. It was sad to see this community come to an end after the roads were built and the boats taken off the river, for all time, and put up on the ways for their retirement."

There was a wood camp at Minto, called Finley Beaton's Woodcamp. Old Finley had lost an arm and had a hook on the stump that was left. "That was an ideal thing for piling wood," Chuck said, "He had a great woodpile there, and he'd grab the stick with his good hand and put the hook in the other end and, Bingo, he was in business. Finley sold more wood than anybody. He used a horse for hauling the wood.

"Speaking of horses, there was one old fellow up the Stewart called Heffering, and he and his horse moved in together in the winter time for warmth. I had to go and call on the guy one spring, and I'll tell you...it was something out of this world! Whew...what a character. But these were just some of the things that went on along the river in those days."

Indians used the rivers quite a bit in the summer, Chuck said. "We would often move whole families from creek to creek. They would load up their whole outfit on the barge: their tents, dogs, kids, cookstove and everything. We put them off at the new location, and they'd set up camp there for a while. Sometimes we'd pass booms of logs that some Indian fellows were taking down to Dawson, huge 100 foot rafts with big sweeps on either end. They would bring them up from the Stewart or Pelly rivers. There would be flat places in the middle of the rafts, where they'd have their tents, and cooking stoves, and away they'd go drifting downstream to Dawson. They generally did the rafting in midsummer when it wasn't dark at nights, because they had to watch out for the steamboats coming."

Life on the sternwheelers was a very comfortable one for the crews. They ate the same meals as the tourists did, most of them on the mess deck, and a steward would keep the tables supplied with the very best food available.

The tourists brought a little bit of the outside life to the interior of the Yukon, and the local people loved to travel on the boats. "I have many friends that lived in Dawson, and they say that their holiday began the minute they stepped into the riverboat at the dock. When the boat started upstream, there they were, all the linens and fancy silverware and crystal, and cutlery and glass. The variety of meals on the menu were fantastic considering where they were. There were usually two lounge rooms, an observation lounge in the bow, and a smoking room in the stern. The cabins were pretty small, but they were comfortable and had fresh linen every day. They had a double lower berth, and a single upper, and they would generally accomodate two people. There was no running water, but there was a washstand in the corner of the cabin with a fancy porcelain water jug, which the steward always kept filled with warm or cold water, as required, and a wash basin. You could push the buzzer once for hot water, or twice for cold. Under the washstand was a compartment with a curtain around it, and that was where the 'pot' was kept, in case nature called during the night.

"There were communal bathrooms on deck and if one wanted a bath, you'd let the steward know the night before, and he'd look after it. Normally, if one was going from Dawson to Whitehorse, and wanted a bath, it would be arranged before the boat got above the White River, because it threw out silt which filled the water with sediment. Instead of drying off with a towel, passengers needed a whisk, to whisk the dust off. The river above that, though, was all clear and delightful.

"It was a terrible tragedy, and I felt real anger, when the steamers *Casca* and *Whitehorse* went up in smoke in 1974. Especially knowing that they were ignited. In all that time I worked and lived up there forty-five years all told...there was never a boat caught fire. And we had eight boats up there at times with all those people working on and around them. Never a fire.

"We used to have a president of the White Pass up there in those days, and he was deathly opposed to smoking. His name was Herb Wheeler, and if you ever came as close to the shipyards as the old Cascade laundry, with a cigarette in your hand, man! He could smell them a mile away, and he'd just beat the can off you. It was because of this kind of supervision and curtailment of people's activities that they were able to keep the boats from burning up.

"They tell a good story about Jack Hoyt, when he first came up to the Yukon. First of all he came to Skagway as a boilermaker for the White Pass and Yukon route. The first job he was sent on was to Whitehorse, because he had to superintend the repair on a boiler on one of the river boats. He'd never seen a riverboat. He went into Whitehorse, and checked in at the Regina Hotel, where he had a meal. Then he decided he'd better go down and see what these boats looked like. So he goes down there with a big cigar in his face, smoking away and looking over these river boats. This big chap comes along, very upright, and said, 'Put out that cigar!' 'I'll do no such thing,' replied Hoyt, 'Who the hell are you?' 'Never mind who I am. Put out that cigar. Who the hell are you?' said Wheeler.

"Hoyt said confidently, 'Well, I'm the new boilermaker.' Wheeler shot back, 'Well, I'm the old president of the company. Now put out that cigar!'"

The sternwheelers were all cut off flat at the stern, and the water from the wheels would be pounding against them all the time, so they were fairly noisy. And some of the boats ran the exhaust from the engines through the stack, which created a draft so the fire that was burning in the boiler would burn more efficiently. This would make a puff, puff, puffing sound all the way up the river, and there would be puffs of white smoke coming out the stacks: a very nostalgic memory for Yukoners after the boats were taken off the river.

10

Louis Irvine

---·•◆•·---

There's a race of men that don't fit in,
A race that can't stay still;
So they break the hearts of kith and kin,
And they roam the world at will.
They range the field and they rove the flood,
And they climb the mountain's crest;
Theirs is the curse of the gypsy blood,
And they don't know how to rest.

Robert Service

Louis Irvine was born in Idaho in 1907. His dad and a partner had joined the stampeders in 1889, and brought forty head of horses over the Chilkoot Trail all the way from Montana.

"Their original idea was to take the outfit to Dawson City, and do some freighting. They brought feed, harness, sleighs, packing outfits and everything for the horses. When they got to Log Cabin, they realized the activity was in Atlin, B.C. right then, so they started freighting to Atlin instead. In the spring, they packed wire and insulators in for the Dominion Telegraph Line that was being put in to Telegraph Creek."

After this, Louis' father started his own mining operation in Atlin on Spruce Creek. "He did well at it, too," Louis said, "It was good property, but you know how young fellows are, the money didn't last too long when he went back outside."

In 1910, Mr. Irvine, married with children by then, brought his family up the coast around by Dutch Harbour and St. Michael. They came up the Yukon to the mouth of the Tanana, and on to Fairbanks by steamboat.

"My dad started mining at Esther Creek in Fairbanks in the fall of 1910," he said. "They stockpiled the ore during the winter, and washed it the next spring. There were five partners in the mining venture. They had taken a lay on a piece of property, and by the time they paid the owner his percentage plus all the other expenses, they ended up with about $5000 each, not too bad for a winter's work."

Louis remembers his dad going over to the bank, and coming home with a sack of $20 gold pieces. He dumped them out on the bed, for the family to admire. They moved to Whitehorse then, in 1911, where they had their first ride on a railroad.

One of Louis' first memories was of coming up the Yukon River in a paddlewheeler and passing a big raft with tents and men and horses on it. Someone on the boat yelled and asked them where they were going. They shouted, "To the Iditarod!" They were going down to make their fortune there, on the only highway that existed in those days, the Yukon River.

In 1916, the family moved back to their ranch in Oregon. The very next year he sold it and bought a place in Seattle. They were flooded out and lost everything they owned, Louis said.

"So we headed back to Ketchican, Alaska, and stayed there for the winter, then came back to the Yukon in the spring of 1918. We walked from Carcross, down to Tagish, and from there to what is now Johnson's Crossing." They had four big pack dogs, which were carrying the food on their backs. One day the dogs took off after a moose that came out of the bush, and lost every bit of it. The whole family went three days without anything to eat except for some dried salmon which, fortunately, they had been carrying themselves.

When they got to Teslin River, on their way to Teslin Post, they waited for the SS *Kluane* to show up. This was the boat that Taylor and Drury was running at the time. They stayed there for three days...waiting...then, thinking that it had already gone by and they had missed it, they built a big raft to cross they river. No sooner had they completed this chore, when they heard the old *Kluane* coming around the bend.

"I can remember that time like it was yesterday," said Louis. "It was the 21st of June, 1918, and it happened to be my birthday. Well, we got on the boat and told them we hadn't had anything to eat for a while and the old cook found out it was my birthday and he made me a cake, with candles and all."

The Irvines lived in a cabin just above Teslin Post, trapping and prospecting until 1921, when they moved to Atlin for a year. Louis finally had a chance to get some schooling, but then in 1922, Mr. Irvine decided to check out a mining property near Dease Lake, B.C., in the Cassiar country at French Creek, and Louis got the job of working on a hydraulic drag line at the mine when he was fifteen years old. They stayed on that creek, mining, for four years. "It was a fair living, enough to keep food on the table, anyway," said Louis, "but then the old man got traveling fever again, and decided we should go back to Missouri, God's country, as he called it, and buy a farm. They paid cash for it, and I never worked so hard in my life for so little."

One day when Louis was out in the wood lot cutting wood, he got fed up, threw down his ax, and said, "Dad, if you want my share of the ranch you can have it. I'm heading back to the Yukon." His dad replied, "Wait until I get my bags packed, and I'll be right with you!" So we headed back. "Mother had to do a little crying, but he told her, you go ahead and take the farm. You can handle it, hire someone to help you. Of course, she wouldn't stay without us, so we sold the farm. We practically gave it away to get rid of it."

Louis eventually left his father moving from place to place, like the restless gypsy he was, and settled at Lake Laberge. The Yukon was to be his home for the rest of his life.

In Louis' day, there were a lot of people living at Laberge, he said. It was the main Indian village for miles around. "Old Dutch Henry had his home on one side of the lake, and on the other was Jim Boss, who was chief of the Laberge Indians, before Whitehorse even existed. Dutch ran a roadhouse for people who were going to Dawson City in the winter months, and fed his guests whitefish, which he called Lake Laberge turkey. He also supplied the riverboats with hundreds of pound of fish, every year.

"Jim Boss was quite a character," Louis said. "He had three wives (at the same time) one of them stayed in the cabin with Jim, and the others had a separate cabin to live in. He also had bunkhouses for river travelers. During the gold rush there were a lot of people traveling on Lake Laberge, and some of them would pay for a bunkhouse to save setting up camp for the night. The others who camped along the beach in their tents would be greeted by Chief Jim Boss upon arising. He would collect fifty cents from each of them for the use of 'his beach.' And Cheechakos (the term for people new to the country) who were not wise to the game would be asked to chip in twenty-five cents, just for stopping their boats to make a meal for themselves."

Old Jim lived and prospered to a ripe old age. He had been living in Whitehorse for quite some time when he died, in 1948, and his friends brought his body back to his old home, and buried him at the Laberge cemetary, at Horse Creek.

Louis Irvine freighted for T. C. Richards, on the river for six winters. He took the mail and freight to the roadhouse at the old junction (where the Stewart river bridge is today). He was met there by the mail carriers from Mayo, and the ones from Dawson (which was 120 river miles from there). The Dawson carriers would pick up the Mayo and Whitehorse mail at this junction; then turn around and head back to Dawson City. Passengers were sometimes taken this way, too.

"Once in a while in the spring, we'd leave Whitehorse with about fifty or sixty passengers on sleds pulled by three Cats, and go all the way to Dawson." Louis said. "It was quite a trip. I remember one time we had two Cats and three drivers, and none of us got any sleep. We were just about dead by the time we got there, from lack of sleep. Matter of fact I did fall asleep once, driving the Cat—close to Discovery Pup—and went off the trail. But as soon as the Cat started to hit that loose snow, I woke up pretty quick."

The drivers didn't have too much trouble keeping the Cats going, as long as they didn't stop. They kept the radiators covered to keep the heat in.

They were freighting to Yukon Crossing and Mayo Junction. There was a period, while the ice was still too thin for travel, that the mail service would sometimes be delayed for a short time. Louis said, "Of course, there were no bridges in those days, so we had to pull the sleigh load over the rivers by hand in the fall, because the ice wasn't strong enough to hold the Cats. We generally worked a crew there to help until the ice got solid enough to go across with the Cats. The first year I was on that trail, it averaged fifty below zero for a whole month.

Stan Rickenson and Louis pulled in to Pelly Crossing one night, and the thermometer there registered seventy-eight below.

That same night, the thermometer at the Selkirk telegraph station registered eighty degrees below zero. "That was the coldest I've ever been out in," Louis said. "In that kind of weather it's like pulling your sled through sand. You can hear them squealing for a mile, those steel runners against that cold snow, and sometimes you would pass by a spruce tree, and it would go off like a pistol shot, just cracking open in the cold. There was very little snow that year, I remember. You couldn't get off and walk behind the Cat for some exercise, because your lungs wouldn't stand the exertion in that cold. So we stood up on the back of the sleigh, periodically, and pulled a big buffalo robe over our heads, and kicked our feet and slapped our hands, to keep up the circulation." Luckily, they didn't have any passengers that trip, because they probably would have frozen.

One time, Louis said, they got to Pelly roadhouse with a man on board who was going to Dawson City. There was nobody running the roadhouse at that time, so they stopped, got a fire going, and went out to get some snow to melt for drinking water. The fellow said to Louis, I've got a bottle of rum in my suitcase, and I think this is rum time if you know where it is. "You bet I do!" answered Louis. So he went out and brought it in. "I'll never forget what that guy said. He opened the suitcase, and darned if he didn't have a thermometer in there. He looked at it and said, 'Oh my god, it's 65 below in my suitcase!' Well, we poured the overproof rum, and it was so cold it was just like pouring molasses."

The Caterpillar train pulled two sleds behind, and had a kerosene lantern tied on the back of the last one, so the drivers could look back and see the reflection of it on the snow when it was dark. This trip, they looked back and couldn't see any light back there. The coal oil was so stiff it couldn't creep up the wick and all the lantern could manage was a faint little blue spark in temperatures that low.

The Cat trains carried eggs and oranges without too much trouble, by burying them in crates of hay and wrapping buffalo robes around them. They carried a lot of beef, too. T. C. Richards owned the one and only butcher shop in Whitehorse, plus the largest hotel in town, the Whitehorse Inn. He also had the contract for the freight and mail haul, so he made sure that no one in Mayo went short of sides of beef for the winter.

A man by the name of Olaf King had the roadhouse at Montague and he kept it warm and ready for the Cat drivers at all times with the coffee always on. "It wasn't easy to leave that nice hot wood heater, when it came time to go." said Louis.

In later years, they started using big R D 6-3 cylinder Cats for the mail run, which were huge compared to the previous ones. They had cabs on them, and could pull a caboose behind the sleds. It was much easier to keep warm after that, and the drivers could even cook themselves a meal.

When the White Pass put in airplanes, said Louis, it spelled the end to the overland trails in the wintertime. Bush pilots could take over after that.

Louis hauled the mail in the spring and fall of 1936, on a boat owned by T. C. called the *Shamrock* before the steamboats had started for the summer, and after they stopped, in the fall. Frankie Slim was his pilot. The Shamrock, loaded with mail, met the last steamship of the season on its way to the ways in

Whitehorse. From then on, she was the mail carrier, until the ice on the river made it impossible to continue. The *Shamrock* was a gasoline-driven launch, a tunnel boat with a Model A marine conversion. She was forty-five feet long and not too fast. Going upstream, the best she could do was five miles an hour and fourteen was the limit for downstream. The last fall Louis ran that boat, he kept track of the miles he and Fred Boss had put in after the river boats had quit for the season: it totaled 1,812 miles. "I was the captain and cook," he said, "and Fred Boss and Frankie Slim were the pilots."

The last fall they ran the *Shamrock*, in 1937, Fred and Louis got into Dawson City on the 8th of November. When they got in sight of Dawson, they started blowing the siren on the launch for all they were worth so they would be noticed, because the ice was forming on the river and it was very hard to maneuvre. They finally eased the boat around, and worked it over to the shore as much as they could. When they got below Dawson, there were some men on one of the docks, standing and waiting for them. Louis threw a 'heaving line' out as hard as he could. About five feet of it landed out on the ice and the men got a hold on it.

"They tied a long, half-inch Manila rope to it," Louis said, "and there were so many guys there, pulling on that rope that I was afraid it would break. I told them to just kind of hold it, until we could work it with the motor, as well. The bad thing about those tunnel boats is that the tunnel will fill up with slush ice, and then you can't do a darn thing with them, except to reverse the motor and try to kick it out that way. Then you can have another go at it. But we finally worked it in to shore." They should have pulled it out of the water right then, because the next morning there was a sheet of four-inch ice all around it. They had to cut around the whole forty-five-foot length of the boat to get rid of the ice. Then they put a cradle under her, and hauled it out of the river.

"T. C. Richards had the winter mail service for fourteen years," Louis said. Even after the airplanes took over most of the business, and White Pass was flying the mail to Dawson, T. C. still ran a Cat train into Mayo, until the winter of 1938-39.

Louis went on a trip downriver to Coffee Creek, once after that, on the SS *Keno*. Keopke was the boss for White Pass Construction at the time, and he had asked Louis if he'd like to go on a nice vacation. There was a mining outfit up above Coffee Creek and the White Pass had sold them a Cat which had broken down. So they sent them another one, and wanted to bring the original back to Whitehorse for repairs. But there wasn't anyone there that knew how to repair a diesel Cat. Keopke told Louis all he'd have to do was go and get that Cat started.

It would be sitting there on the bank, he said, so they could load it right onto the boat. "Then you can go to on to Dawson City...and we're going up to Scroggie Creek to pick up some stuff on the Stewart, so you'll have a real picnic," he told him. "That sounds pretty good to me," said Louis.

When they got off at Coffee Creek, Ned Boss was there to meet him. Louis looked around for the Cat, but it was nowhere in sight, so he asked Ned about it. "Oh, heck, that thing is about thirteen miles up the mountain in a mud hole, with the tracks off it." Ned told him.

"There went my holiday, right there," Louis said, "I had to go way back in the bush with him. We finally got the tracks back on it, three days later. Old Nick the Greek, a fellow that was around Whitehorse for years, had been working at the mine and he was quitting, so he came down as far as the Cat that Ned and I were working on. He helped me bring it down to the river bank. We noticed that there was a lot of yellow dirt on the tracks when we got it there, and I thought I'd pan some of it and see how many 'colors' I could find." Louis cleaned out an old washbasin he found in the willows, and tried his luck. Mixed with the black sand in the bottom of the pan he found a nice showing of yellow gold. He then went to work and bulldozed a nice ramp for loading the Cat, and when the SS *Keno* came back for it they just had to put out a couple of planks and drive the Cat right on. Louis and Nick walked on behind it, and the boat left for Whitehorse. Louis: "That was the day they dropped the first atomic bomb on Hiroshima, because I heard about it on the radio, that day on the *Keno*."

For lack of anything else to do, he said, he asked some of the deckhands if they'd ever panned for gold. None of them had, so Louis said, "Well, you get a tub of water out here, I'll clean one of these washbasins out and show you how it's done." When they saw the colors in the pan they wanted to know if they could try. "Sure!" Louis told them, "Go ahead." By the time they got to Whitehorse, there wasn't a speck of dirt left in those Cat tracks. And all the fellows had a few pennyweights of gold in their watch pockets to take back to Vancouver. "They were as pleased as punch," Louis said. "They'd be able to brag to their friends back home about the gold they'd panned in the Klondike. And the guys in the White Pass garage in Whitehorse were happy because cleaning the dirt from Cat tracks wasn't one of their favorite jobs either."

"It's a lonesome old river, now." said Louis. "Once in a while you'll see some people going down on a raft or something, but everything's gone. Cabins that you could see sitting out there, you just don't see them anymore. Yep, she's a lonesome old river."

11

Johnny Hogan

The river springs like a racer, sweeps through a gash in the
rock;
Butts at the boulder-ribbed bottom, staggers and reels at the
shock;
Leaps like a terrified monster, writhes in its fury and pain;
Then with the crash of a demon, springs to the onset again.

Robert Service

Johnny Hoggan's father was a deep sea skipper before coming to the Yukon. He ran scows and rafts through the Whitehorse rapids for the gold seekers, during the gold rush. In later years he went into the Kluane country on a stampede. When that proved to be unsuccessful, the family moved to Whitehorse for a while (where Johnny was born in 1903).

Captain John Hoggan Sr. went to work for White Pass on their steamboats along the Yukon River. While still employed with the company, he moved his family to Hootalinqua, where they lived during the years 1911 until 1916. In the winter months, Captain Hoggan acted as caretaker for the ships that were stored there until spring. These smaller steamboats were used on the Stewart River, to haul the ore from Mayo. In 1911, there was only one wintered there, the SS *Canadian*. Two years later the *Yukon* and *Alaska* were among his charges as well.

The White Pass supplied the groceries for the families in their employ, in those years, and they ordered whatever they would be needing during the coming winter from the big commissary in Whitehorse. In the line of meat, they were allowed (for each man) a side of beef, 1 whole pig, a case of bacon, plus 5 cases of milk, 6 or 7 sacks of flour, 200 lbs. of sugar, and so on. These were the rations allowed—per man— for the winter. The supplies were shipped to them in the fall. The snow acted as a deep-freeze in the winter months, and in the summer they depended on the country for their fresh meat and vegetable supply.

Johnny, with his two brothers and a sister, put in the summers wandering around the country. Their closest permanent neighbors were at Lower Laberge, thirty miles away. From the middle of October, until mid-March, they never saw another white person. About thirty miles up the Hootalinqua River (now called the Teslin) was a place where the mail stage went through to Livingstone Creek. Johnny and his sister took their dog teams up the river once a month, to meet the stage and pick up the mail. "Just for something to do," said Johnny, "we'd go up one day and back the next. Otherwise, if he didn't see us there, the fellow from Big Salmon would bring it over for us when he came to pick up his own mail."

A few Indian families had cabins close by, and Johnny learned to speak their language as well as they could. The kids all played together, but in the winter time the Indian families would go off trapping, and the Hoggans would be alone again. Indian families always moved to wherever there was game available, never staying in one place for very long. When someone shot a moose, they moved their tents to that spot and lived there for a while. It was easier than packing the moose out of the bush. This activity was typical of their lifestyle at the time.

The Indians smoked fish during the summer months, in 'fish camps' along the river. It was a food source for themselves and their dogs in the winter time, along with the smoked and dried wild meat.

Johnny said he was never lonely. "We had a wonderful life, I don't think I'd trade my boyhood for anyone else I ever knew. In the summer we had a little poling boat, and although I was only about twelve years old (my sister was two years older), we used to pole way up the river, line the boat up the Hootalinqua, and we'd be gone a whole week sometimes. There was a good place to hunt grouse up at 17 Mile, and we picked a lot of berries there, too. Sometimes we would just go across the river, and walk up the telegraph line to Livingstone Creek."

They walked about twenty miles up the line to a place called Mason's Landing, picking berries, shooting rabbits and grouse, and just living off the country. When they got tired of that, they would build a raft out of three or four logs and drift home.

"We never thought anything of it," Johnny said. "Nowadays, you never go anywhere without a life preserver on. We'd just take two or three little logs and hammer a couple of paddles out of some trees, and away we'd go; sometimes sitting on the logs with our feet dangling in the water. My folks never worried about it either, because they were used to it, I guess. We did it from the time we were small. My sister and I had a dog team each, and in the winter we went hunting and trapping. I packed a rifle from the time I was big enough to drag it over the ground."

Johnny's formal schooling consisted of a couple of months one summer in Skagway, and one winter (1908-09) in Whitehorse, and then in 1914, he went to school in Dawson for several months. The youngest Hoggan girl was sent outside to school in 1912, to Shawnigan Lake on Vancouver Island. When she came home in the summertime, she taught her brothers.

The kids' father was on the riverboats in the summer months, and their mother seemed quite content with life as it was. There were no other women there, until Johnny's two older half-sisters came over from England in 1912. (One of them married a telegraph operator, and stayed in the country until 1927.)

The shipyard at Hootalinqua was built in 1913, when the White Pass built the SS *Yukon* and the *Alaska* and put them on the lower river run, which was Northern Commercial's exclusive run before that.

For a while there was a rate war on. A person could book a passage from Dawson to Whitehorse for five dollars, first class. In the end, neither company was making any money, and the White Pass eventually bought the NC out for $3 million. It was during this period that the White Pass purchased a number of boats from the lower river run, including the *Susie, Sarah, Tanana,* and the SS *Norcom,* which was renamed the *Evelyn.*

A year later Johnny's family moved to Dawson City. John Hoggan Sr. worked at Sunnydale Slough, which was another place where the White Pass stored boats for the winter. Among the vessels in his care were big boats from the lower, or Alaskan section of the Yukon River.

Johnny worked on the paddlewheelers, starting at the age of fourteen, from 1917 to 1921. He worked on the steamers *Dawson, Casca, Hazel B* and *Sybilla,* and went from deckhand to purser to pilot. During those years he went to school in the winter months, and finished his grade ten.

Johnny worked along with Cam Smith and Emil Forrest, and he made trips on the lower river into Alaska delivering mail to Nenana and a place called Holycross. Then he switched to the steamer *Whitehorse* which went along the upper river.

Hoggan remembers when cattle were being driven over the Dawson trail, from Whitehorse to Carmacks. At Carmacks, they were loaded onto three-deck cattle barges, for transfer to Dawson. The cattle rode on the lower deck; pigs and sheep were loaded on the middle; geese, chickens, and turkeys on the upper deck. If you happened to be on one of the boats pushing those barges, you just hoped the wind would be blowing the right way, otherwise the smell from all that livestock would be overpowering. "It would take two or three trips before you'd get all that smell off the barge," said Johnny. "It was terrible!"

Kirkman Creek was a bad spot in the river; there was a sand bar where the boats often had trouble. Everyone was afraid of an old woodcutter who lived there, too. The story was told that he could put a curse on the boats, and if he did, they would get stuck every time they passed through that channel. The old man used to measure his own wood, and would usually come up short of the actual figure. If anyone argued about it, he would make the boat crew put the wood back on the bank. He would then put a curse on the boat. And if it got stuck on the bar, the boat would have to come back and pay his price for the wood, because they'd be running out of steam for the boilers.

Summertime was a time for visiting, if you had a boat. You could go away for a week at a time, and never dream of locking your cabin. Nothing ever got stolen in those days. "Not at all like today," said Johnny Hoggan.

There used to be thousands of cords of wood rafted down the Yukon River in the summertime to Dawson City. Some cords were taken all the way from Five Finger Rapids on huge rafts with large sweeps (paddles) on both ends. Some of the fellows who had been cutting all winter had ninety cords of four-foot and six-foot wood on board. Many Indian woodcutters used this method of earning a livelihood.

There were usually four men to each raft. They steered them down to Dawson, drifting with the current, and then had to hitch a ride up river again, where they made another one. "We were passing rafts on the river all the time," said Johnny. "They cut wood along that river for fifty years, but today you can't see any signs of it at all."

Johnny and his brothers carried mail from Coffee Creek to Dawson, for a number of years, by dog team. They made a trip once a month. It could be tough on the river when there was a storm, the weather extremely cold, and the trail all drifted in. In the fall, when the ice was running, they would have to switch to the overland route.

Johnny: "I was also on the mail run with Louis Irvine for two years, driving a Cat from Stewart Junction to Dawson. Junction was inland, on the Dawson Trail. When the White Pass ran the mail, we used to get three stages a week into Dawson. But after they lost the contract, we'd only get our mail once every fifteen days. Most of the time, the second class stuff

155

would be stockpiled, because of the weight. When the first steamboat of the season came into Dawson, it would be loaded with only second class mail. There would be catalogues and newspapers from way back in the fall.

"Norman Ryder, Louis Moi, George Howatt, Stan Rickenson, Sam Wood, Len Thompson and Sandy Yeulet, were all mail carriers. They would run alternately...one week Louis and I would meet Norman and Sandy at the Junction, and take the mail from there to Dawson, and maybe the next time it would be Stan and Len meeting us there instead. They came every two weeks, because they had farther to go. I could make my run in five and a half days, to Dawson and back."

Johnny took a trip down the river in his own boat, many years later.

"It gave me a real strange feeling," he said, "all the old places were gone, the river channels have changed, and you begin to realize that to most people now it's just a stream of water running through the country. How many people actually know the real history of what went on along that river in the early days? Not too many, I think. It's sad to think of it."

12

Ed Whitehouse

---◆---

His Majesty's Mail

We've been running all day, on this rough frozen lake.
The dogs pull the sleigh, but my legs—how they ache!
The dogs' feet are sore, I can tell by their wail,
But we have to deliver His Majesty's mail.

We're reaching the shore line, I think we'll rest here.
We're not behind schedule...there's nothing to fear.
I kindle a camp fire, and get the dogs fed,
Then pull down some spruce boughs to serve as a bed.

My buffalo robe is worn and it's old—
No longer able to keep out the cold.
Howling away at the moon big and bright,
Why are my Husky's so restless tonight?

The long night has ended, we mush on our way.
The post is in sight now...they heave on the sleigh.
Their steps start to quicken, they're wagging their tail,
For they know they've delivered His Majesty's mail.

Joyce Yardley

Ed Whitehouse was born in Dawson City on January 2, 1909. Dawson was much larger than it is today. It boasted a population of several thousand, had four barber shops and had seven hotels.

Steamboats from Fairbanks used to come into Dawson on the lower river, as the Alaskan portion of the Yukon River was called. These steamers met the boats from Whitehorse, and exchanged passengers, so that meant several hundred tourists a week came into Dawson. The tourist industry in the Yukon was thriving, even in those days.

"My dad left England with 200 other adventurers, on a chartered boat, and came all the way to the mouth of the Yukon River, via the Panama Canal, in 1898," said Ed. "Included in the cargo of that ship was a steam yacht, which belonged to my dad and uncle. They launched it at St. Michael, and came into Dawson that way." The name of the boat was the *Wyburn*, and it was wrecked on the Snake River in Alaska, in 1901. It drew too much water to be used in the upper Yukon, so they sold it to another Englishman, who took it down the lower river to its resting place on the Snake.

Ed: "Those men brought everything with them to the Klondike goldfields. In fact, I still have my dad's double-barrelled elephant rifle, which he brought into the country!"

In 1909, there were roads to 60 Mile, Bonanza, Horse, Dominion, Quartz, Gold Run and Rock Creek, and pack trails all over the hills. The furthest you could drive with a car, though, was to Rock Creek. "Unless it was very, very dry," Ed said, "and then you could make it out to North Fork, to the power plant."

No one in Dawson had any radios until the early 1930s. "We had one," Ed said. "We used to get KDK in Pittsburg, and one station in San Francisco. Lots of people came over to our cabin at night just to listen to the radio. There was only one other in Dawson, and another at 60 Mile, so ours was the second or third radio in Dawson."

Ed worked on the gold dredges for a few years and then, in the winter of 1928-29, he contracted out to the Post Office Department for the mail run between Dawson City, Stewart post office, and up the Stewart River twenty-eight miles, to another post office at Scroggie Creek.

"The White Pass hauled the mail in the summer months, when the going was good, but when it was tough, in the winter, it was up to us old sourdoughs to run it." There were a series of contracts split up into side runs. Percy de Wolf had the one downriver to Eagle, and at Stewart City there was an old fellow by the name of Felix Laderoute, who took over from there using a horse to get to Coffee Creek. (Incidentally, Laderoute was raising domestic sheep at Coffee Creek—probably the only person to ever raise them in the Yukon.) The contracts continued in this fashion, all the way to Whitehorse. They used the rivers whenever they could, cutting across a few 'jutting' points by land (trail permitting) if it saved several miles. Travel was mostly all by dog team during that period of time.

Ed's mail run from Stewart back to Dawson would typically take the following route: at Stewart, there were two hotels and a general store. One of the hotels was run by a lady named Mrs. Shand. Many trappers lived there, including Hughie Charters, Tom Quinn and Scottie Heaver, who worked for the White Pass in the summer; and a very interesting fellow, Anders Cross, who was a Laplander. He had come into the country driving reindeer. Captain Hoggan and his family lived there, as well as several old-timers who trapped and mined the sand bars along the Stewart River.

Harland Slough was the next mail stop, going north. Captain Hanson trapped there in the winter, and was in charge of one of the paddlewheelers in the summer months. He and John Hoggan were two of the very few captains who stayed in the Yukon in the wintertime.

Next came Rosebud, where 'Belgian Joe' Verheldst lived, trapping and mining, followed by Ogilvie Island where the telegraph operator was George Hoggan (a member of Captain Hoggan's family). Louis Cruikshank had a big farm there. He grew his own hay for the big herd of cattle he was raising. Just across the Yukon River from Ogilvie, and on up from there to the mouth of the 60 Mile River, were quite a number of old timers mining, trapping and cutting wood.

"They all seemed to be contented," said Ed, "stayed there the year round. There was lots of wood and moose, and millions of caribou used to migrate through that country. I've been on the boat lots of times when it has had to stop to let the caribou go by. This wasn't the Porcupine herd I'm talking about now, it was the 40 Mile Alaskan herd that used to come through. They were shooting them by the thousands during the construction of the Alaska Highway. I guess the caribou changed their migration route, because they're not around any more like they used to be."

Below Ogilvie Island about four miles, there used to be an old fellow by the name of Smiley. "I remember his cabin well," said Ed. "It was so clean you could eat off the floor. He even dusted the ridge pole on the ceiling. He was a professional welder at the Whitehorse shipyards, and he preferred spending the winters at his cabin, to going back outside until spring came again."

The next major stop was Indian River; George Fair, a fine old gentleman, lived there. He was a Manxman. Ed used to drop the mail off and spend the night in George's cabin. It was the pick-up spot for all the people in the close vicinity: many would cross the river to come and get their mail.

Just below Indian River, at 20 Mile Rock, was a fellow that cut wood for the White Pass, called Archie McCoomb.

Leaving Dawson, in the fall, the mail load would be quite heavy, because of the big orders from the Eatons catalogues coming in. But as a general rule, the weight of the mail would average four or five hundred pounds. People would order heavy clothes, axes, saws, nails and the Dawson newspapers. Not many Vancouver papers were ordered, because they were bunched up in Whitehorse and folks wouldn't get them until spring, when the river boats would bring them a whole mailsack full. It took quite a while to catch up with all the news!

On the return run, there would be some furs and a bundle of letters, and that would be about all. The mail and freight in the winter came from Whitehorse on the overland stage route by horse drawn sled, and later by Caterpillar tractors. And still later, at times, by truck, if the trail was exceptionally good.

Snow conditions could vary from day to day, depending on the temperature.

"I never lost any mail in all the time I was on that haul, but I did go through the ice once," Ed remembered, "thank gosh it was on a return trip. It was early spring, and what had happened was that the swift water underneath had undermined the ice since I'd been over it four days previously. I really knew better, too. You never go near a bar or an island, when you are on ice in the spring, because the water warms up going over the gravel, and cuts the ice away underneath. Well, I was running behind the dogs, not holding onto the handles, and I saw the lead dog's foot go through the ice. First I thought it was just overflow, but by the time I caught up to them, it was down the hatch, sleigh, dogs and all. I hollered to the dogs, and they held on. The sleigh bobbed up and I went hand over hand over the handlebars to the back dog, hollering at them all the time. They were scratching and whining—straining like crazy to get out. I had a small mail pouch on board, which I couldn't reach, and I thought, 'Well, in this case the dogs come first.' I had a small sheath knife, and I thought I'd have to cut the traces on them, because the current was trying to pull them under, but they kept trying, desperately, to pull that sleigh and themselves out of the water. And by God, they did it!

"We had five miles left to go, and it was twenty below zero. I ran as far as I could, until my clothes got so stiff I couldn't run any more. I just flopped on the sleigh, and the dogs took me to George Fair's, at Indian River. I got pneumonia on that trip, and had to hire someone else to make the next one. It was the only run I ever missed."

The mail always ran on schedule, two trips a month. It took Ed eight days, four up and four down. They had to be on time because there was always someone waiting at the other end to relay it along from post to post. "There'd always be some fellow out there on the trail to meet you," said Ed. "If you didn't have any mail for him, you'd have to stop to pass on any news verbally. Who's new in town, how did old Harry make out on

Hunker Creek, and how much fur did Joe bring into the store last month, and so on."

Ed raised his own dogs, for a while—Alaska malamutes. He used five or six dogs in his team, and if he ever needed more, he could rent them for fifty cents a day. He never carried a whip because he didn't believe in using them. But he had to use a whip in Dawson, he said, when so many other dogs were around and sometimes he'd have to break up a dog fight. "I never lost a dog," he said proudly.

Ed also sold a few furs for the trappers along the line. He charged two dollars a skin for selling them. He would take them into Dawson and barter for the best price. There was quite a bit of competition among the six fur buyers there. One winter a new store sprang up on Front Street in Dawson, and the proprietor, who was new to the fur trade, made Ed a deal. "I'd like you to bring the furs to me," he told him. "Well, I can't do that," said Ed, "I have to sell them to the highest bidder." The storekeeper replied, "I'll tell you what I'm going to do. If you go around and find out what the highest bid is—I'll give you two dollars more than that for the trapper, plus two dollars more for you, for every fur that you bring in."

"So I got four dollars extra for every skin that came out of the Stewart country that winter. I took in $4000, which was quite a bit of money in depression times. Of course, the trappers got $2000 extra, too, so it was an honest deal."

Along the trail, he would overnight with the occasional trapper, and at Stewart he stayed at Shand's Hotel. At the end of the line, up the Stewart River, he sometimes visited the Bragga family, who ran the Scroggie Creek roadhouse. All the roadhouses had facilities to keep dogs, little log houses all lined with hay. Ed had to carry his own dog food, usually dried salmon, of which he fed them two pounds day. (The police in Dawson kept fifty dogs for their patrols. Ed said their rations were one and a half pounds per day.) Ed also carried quarter-pound dog biscuits for little treats during the day. "I still love dogs," he said, "and I really looked after my team." The dried salmon would be cooked up with rice, or cornmeal, and fed to them, warm, after the day's work was done. They always ate before Ed did. He used to bring the harnesses inside at night, so they would be all thawed out and soft in the morning. When all the chores were over, he would go into the road-house, where a hot meal would be waiting for him. The going rate for a meal at that time was one dollar, and the same for a bed.

One fall Ed got caught at Galena Creek. The ice had moved, he said, and he couldn't get across it. He remembered seeing an old cabin that was a mile or so away, back in the bush. Because it was getting dark already, and Indian River was still another ten miles away, he went looking for it. He found the cabin all right, but someone had taken the windows out, probably to use in a new one they were building. It was minus thirty, but he always carried a good eiderdown sleeping bag in his survival kit, so he managed to keep warm for the night. The next morning it was a lot easier to make his way between the patches of open water in the creek. Ed always carried his bedroll, an ax, some hardtack, sardines and a billy can for making tea over a campfire. "And doughnuts," he said. "Doughnuts were great for keeping your energy up because they're cooked in grease, and you could eat them when they were still frozen."

Ed always felt reasonably safe, out on the trail. "For one thing," he said, "you always knew that if you broke a leg or anything, you'd just have to climb in the sled, and those dogs would take you back home. Besides that, everyone looked out for everyone else, on the river. They knew you were coming, and if you didn't get there when they expected, they would go looking for you. At daylight, the morning after I slept in that cabin, I met a fellow coming down the river, looking for me!"

And often Ed would meet one of the RCMP officers on patrol. "They were always out on the river, they patrolled continu-ally. Used to go way back into that White River country. I used to run into Sergeant Cronkite a lot. I remember seeing his dog team way over in the distance, one time, and as they got closer, the dogs began making a big wide detour around me. I couldn't figure out what was going on—until they stopped right across the river from me, and Cronkite yelled over, 'Several of my dogs have distemper, and we don't want yours to catch it.' I figured that was pretty thoughtful of him. He lost a couple of dogs on that trip."

The police especially kept track of all the old-timers. "I remember one time they went out on the Ridge Road, and shot 200 caribou. Not one thing was wasted, they saved the skins, horns, everything. Came in and hauled them out with horse teams, and went up the creeks (Dominion and Sulphur) and gave the old-timers meat for the winter."

There were no Indian people along the mail run, or at Stewart and Ogilvie, at all. Ed said they were at Moosehide and up the Peel and White rivers, and around Snag.

"That's in the Dawson area, I'm talking about now," he said.

"In my single days," said Ed, "I used to take a couple of weeks off in the winter, and go to Vancouver. My friends and I would bypass Whitehorse, and go right on through to Skagway, on the train. That's where all the action was, while we were waiting to catch the coast boat. Whitehorse was too quiet for us in those days."

Although Dawson City was Ed's home town, he eventually moved to Whitehorse, where he lived out the rest of his life—a true Yukoner at heart.

13

Hymie Koshevoy

————•◆•———

The summer—no sweeter was ever;
The sunshiny woods all athrill;
The grayling aleap in the river,
The Bighorn asleep on the hill.

Robert Service

Hymie Koshevoy was thumbing through the Vancouver newspaper one morning in 1928, when an ad in the job opportunity section caught his eye. It stated that the White Pass and Yukon Route were needing crew members for their riverboats in Canada's Yukon Territory. Hymie wanted to become a journalist, and was working his way through university in Vancouver at the time. "I jumped at the chance," he said, "because it wasn't everyday that a student like myself could find a job that paid sixty dollars a month, found. I made enough money in two years to pay my university fees and keep me in comfort for the rest of the year. Three hundred dollars a season doesn't sound like much now, but then it went a long way; and it kept me in the little luxuries of life, such as cigarettes, school meals, books and fees." A friend of Hymie's, Malcolm McGregor, was going up to work with his father, who was a pantryman on one of the steamboats. Malcolm was promised the job of waiter, and he suggested that Hymie go with him.

Hymie: "Mr. Wheeler was the boss of White Pass in those

days, he only had one eye, but he was a sort of god of the Yukon because whoever had anything to do with the Yukon had to deal with the White Pass. Mr. Redpath was the port boss, and Mr. Gordon was the general manager. Malcolm and I signed on the same way we would have done if we had signed onto a deep sea vessel. We had to swear allegiance to Her Majesty, the Queen."

Their first job was to get the boat ready for the first trip of the season. The ice wasn't quite out of Lake Laberge at the time. Crews were spreading lamp black on the ice to speed up the melting process, they called it The Lamp Black Trail. (Mr. Wheeler had come up with this idea of mixing lamp black and old crank-case oil. It worked quite well.) When the first paddlewheeler got to Lake Laberge, it smashed its way though the shell ice for two or three miles, and then the crew could see the coal black trail stretching ahead, way off into the distance. Apparently, this lamp black had the ability to attract the rays of the sun and when the boat suddenly came in contact with this black trail, the water parted. "Just like the red sea," said Hymie, "the ship went right through it like mush. It was a curious episode indeed." The current in the main river could now clear it of ice—two weeks earlier than it would normally take.

Laberge was just like a great big skating rink, just before the ice went out. Later in the season, though, if a strong wind came up, it could be like a little sea. And 30 Mile River was the most dangerous part of the whole trip. It was a winding, twisting, snakelike river, with canyons and a tremendous force of water going through it. It was a great danger to these flat-bottomed boats, and quite often it broke them up.

"I've seen a boat forced into the bank there, by the power of the 30 Mile. And I've seen a big barge break right loose from the steamship. When this happened, they'd have a terrible time getting hold of the thing again and tying it back up. Then they'd have to get it back in position to go up the river again.

"I found the Yukon to be a fascinating place." said Hymie, "I had always heard about 'the call of the Yukon,' but I never really believed it...until after I left there. I began to feel the urge to go back. It was such a beautiful country. After I finished my dish-washing chores on the boat, I'd go out and sit on the barge we were pushing and dangle my legs over the edge, and watch the beautiful scenery unroll. Sometimes I'd see thousands of caribou crossing the river, other times there would be a bear roaming the hills; there was always something exciting to watch. We had lovely weather, and we weren't bothered by the mosquitoes on the boat. Just coursing down the river, with a soft wind in your face, and all that majestic scenery unfolding before you."

Hymie had a lot of dishes to wash, and he used dozens of dish towels during a shift. It made for a lot of laundry, and one day he got a bright idea. Watching that big paddle wheel going around and around, he thought, "What a good washing machine that would make." He got hold of enough rope to reach out beyond the wake from those churning paddles, tied it to a laundry bag which he had filled with dish cloths, and then tied the other end to the ship. The bundle of laundry was bobbing merrily along in the water, behind the paddlewheel, and Hymie was very delighted, because soon he'd have a bundle of nice white dish cloths to use. An hour later, he went back to find that the thin rope had snapped, and the dish cloths were nowhere to be seen. Never at a loss for very long, Hymie devised another idea. He went into the linen closet and filched a couple of bed sheets, which he tore into nice large dish cloths, much to the anguish of the chief steward Mr. James. He was a tall, lean, forbidding man, who didn't take very kindly to pranks of any sort on the ship.

Hymie was in some awe of the officers, being a youngster at the time, because they were in control of the ship. Finally, though, he got friendly with one of the pilots, who let him steer the boat for a short time to let him get the feel of the wheel. "I felt just like Mark Twain on the Mississippi; here I was in command of a giant sternwheeler, and it was quite a thrill for a young man," said Hymie.

He worked on the SS *Whitehorse* first, then he went over to Carcross and worked on the *Tutshi* which ran the length of Tagish Lake, to a tourist attraction at the end, called Ben-My-

Chree. An elderly couple, hired by White Pass, entertained the tourists with dandelion wine, tea cakes and a singsong around the piano.

There was a small railroad at Scotia Bay, which joined Tagish Lake to Atlin Lake, where the train was met by another boat that took people to the town of Atlin, B.C., across the lake. Most of the passengers didn't want to go to Atlin, they just wanted to have a look at the little railway. Those that did want to go, could do so, and some of the crew went to Atlin by this route, on their days off.

There were two ex-convicts working on the *Tutshi*, the year Hymie was on that run. They thought they were pretty tough, and one day when the boat was docked in Carcross, they got into a fight with each other on the freight deck, much to the dismay of some of the citizens there. There was a skipper on the boat, whom they called Black Mac, a big, powerful man. Somebody called him, and he came down and said, "What's going on here?" They told him that these two men wouldn't stop fighting, so he took them both by the scruff of the neck, cracked their heads together, and hurled them bodily off the boat. That was the end of those two men. They had lost their jobs right there.

It seems strange, in these days of labor relations, that an argument could be settled so quickly, and so finally. "Today, there would be grievances and appeals and who knows what, but back then it was 'off the ship and back to Vancouver.'"

The American tourists were enthralled by the paddle-wheelers; the waiters would act as tour guides and entertain them with tall tales. They enjoyed the atmosphere of the boats and the meals, and the excellent service.

The next boat Hymie worked on was the SS *Klondike*. He tells a story of going to a silent movie in Dawson one time with some of the crew. They were sitting there in the theater, with quite a few of the local townfolk, watching a show called, *The Lily of the Valley*, when someone came in with a message that they'd have to leave; the sailing time of the steamboat had been changed for some reason. So they had to get up and go in the middle of the movie.

The next week they were back in town, and went to the movie house again. The proprietor recognized them and said, "Oh, you were the fellows that were here last week, and had to leave. Where did you leave off?" They told him the part in the plot that they had missed, and he went and dug out the reel, put it on, and fast forwarded it to the section they had been watching a week earlier, and they got to see the finish of the film that way.

Hymie was intrigued when he found out that the all the prints of the movies that were sent up north, never went out again. It wasn't worth the cost to send them back, so they all piled up into a big empty room in an old saloon.

Hymie: "The proprietor had hundreds of old movies in boxes back there. He had an old gramophone for background music, and strangely enough, he liked Hawaiian music. So here we were, way up near the arctic circle, watching an ancient movie, with the gramophone droning out 'Twilight Shadows are Calling, Calling me Back to Hawaii.'"

The paddlewheelers had sort of an up and down movement, Hymie said. "It was like a constant shake, but it was quite restful, the slap of the paddles put you to sleep every night, and you weren't bothered by them at all."

In 1930, Hymie tried to go back to the Yukon, but they didn't need his services then. He never did get back, much to his regret, "because you grow to love the Yukon, once you get up there."

14

Len Usher and Charlie Randall

———•◆•———

We watched the groaning ice wrench free,
Crash on with a hollow din;
Men of the wilderness were we,
Freed from the taint of sin.

Robert Service

Captain Charlie Coghlin was the one who persuaded Len Usher to come to the Yukon, in 1948. Len worked as deckhand the first year, on the SS *Aksala*. He put in five years altogether on the *Aksala*, *Keno*, *Nasutlin*, *Casca* and *Klondike*, going from fireman, in the first year, to second mate. While on the SS *Keno*, he put in three years on the Stewart River, hauling silver ore from Mayo to Stewart City.

The job of fireman was a tough one. The large boats burned about a cord an hour. The fireman's job was four hours on and eight off. In a four-hour shift, they would have to stuff four cords of wood into the firebox. The wood was in four-foot lengths on the smaller boats, and six-foot for the larger ones. Some of it was left as round logs, and some would have to be split. And a lot of it was burned black. "You really earned your wages, at that job," said Len. "It was hotter than blazes down there. I never experienced anything quite as hot as when you opened the old firebox, and that blast hit you. I had a fairly good watch, that I used to wear in my watch pocket.

It curled up and quit that fall, and I blamed the heat from that boiler. And to add insult to injury, you'd be as black as tar at the end of your shift, from handling all that burnt wood."

The riverboats never stopped on their voyage upstream, except for wood or freight. They traveled all night. Most of the crew's quarters were in the extreme stern of the boat. On one side was the engine room, and on the other was the transom of the boat, with the paddlewheel right behind it. The rooms were small, and there were four men to a room, in bunks.

Len: "I never had any trouble sleeping. Actually it was pretty soothing there, with the sound of the engines and the paddlewheels thumping right beside your head. I slept well and I think most of the boys did. It was loud enough so there wasn't much conversation in our quarters back there when we were running, because you couldn't hear. But it didn't stop you from sleeping, for some reason." The paddles made quite a distinctive sound. You could hear each bucket plank hitting the water, sort of a thump, thump, thump sound, which varied depending on the speed the boat was traveling. Some of the men, such as the purser, first mates, skippers and so on, had better accommodations on the upper decks, and they had steam radiators for heating.

Everyone had access to a shower, but apart from that, the facilities were not what you would call modern. Doing laundry involved the fellows using a plunger in a galvanized tub, and for heavier items, such as jeans, they utilized the soogie brush, that was used for scrubbing down the decks. They would simply lay the jeans down on the freight deck and scrub the dirt out of them with that brush.

The boats carried fifteen to twenty-five crew members, depending on boat size, consisting of a captain, pilot, first mate, second mate, a purser and three engineers: chief, second and third. There were three firemen, a chef and second cook, and four stewards, plus five to eight deckhands.

When the tourists arrived in Whitehorse, on the train from Skagway, they were escorted right onto their berth on the boat. Ten days later, the steamer brought the tourists back as well as pushing a barge, loaded with freight and ore.

Len was first mate on watch with the skipper and the pilot. Mates normally worked twelve hours on and had twelve hours off, and the pilot and skippers worked six hours on and six off. It was the responsibility of the mate to oversee landings, when the boat was pulling in to pick up wood or mail, and see that the outfit was tied up and the planks brought out for loading the wood on to the boat. Sometimes the boats had to line up at two or three places along the river, and always at Five Finger Rapids, and the mate would oversee that, too.

A wire cable (an inch and a quarter in diameter) was installed at the various rapids—Five Fingers in particular—for those boats needing help to buck the current going upstream. The top part of the end hung in the river with a float on it to assist the crew to pick it up with a pike pole. The boats approached the rock banks and maneuvered in close enough to pick up the floater cable, which was hauled by hand through "snatch blocks" and then connected to the steam winches, or capstans, depending on which the boat had. Now the steamer was hanging on the cable, and the winch would pull it through the rapids.

They made stops at all the creeks along the river. There was always someone living at these places, in addition to the larger centres of Minto, Carmacks, Selkirk and Stewart.

The last trip of the season could be a scary one. Len was on the *Nasutlin* one fall, when the river was running ice. They pulled out in the morning to test the water, and decided to risk going on. But when they got upstream a few miles, the ice plugged up the water intake for the boiler pumps. So they had to back down...all the way to Dawson. The *Nasutlin* never got out of Dawson again. An attempt was made to pull the steamer out: a crew stayed there, for about a week, building a set of makeshift ways for the boat. Then a couple of big Cats were brought in from the creeks, and they tried to slide her out of the water, but it was not a success. The stern strap broke, causing the stern to sink back into the water. So they left her there, half in and half out of the water, and that is where she spent the winter.

In the spring, the run-off from the ice broke her up, and

that was the end of the *Nasutlin*. The only thing that was salvaged was the wheelhouse, and it now sits in an outdoor museum in Dawson City.

The boats were fragile in some ways, and in others they were incredibly tough, when you consider the abuse they could take, such as being dragged over the sandbars, over-loaded with freight, and frozen in the ice at times. They were built light, to keep down the weight on the upper decks. A run of ice could clean the housework (anything above the lower deck) right off a boat that was in shallow water. They had to be shallow draft, because of the sandbars. The smaller ones, such as the *Keno*, would draw four feet of water. And the very largest—six feet, at the most. This was with a load. Sitting light, they only drew a foot and a half, or two feet of water.

At one point in the riverboat era, dance excursions became popular. The White Pass used one of the boats, hooked a barge up to her, all rigged up with a clean canvas floor, pulled taut and waxed. They would hire an orchestra for the evening, and the passengers were treated to an evening of dancing, as the paddlewheeler took them on a trip to Upper Laberge, and back.

And in 1952, for a short period, the *Klondike* was used for an excursion boat. It was set up with a bar, a little dance floor (on the freight deck at that time) and an orchestra. The route was the same to Lake Laberge and back.

Len Usher and his wife took a trip downriver in June of 1979. They started out from Johnsons Crossing, and went down the Teslin River, all the way to Carmacks. "There were a lot of changes." Len said, "I was looking for wood-camps and buildings, but they're very hard to pick out now, because the trees have grown up so much. Everything looks different. For instance, at Big Salmon—as I remember it—there was a big clearing there, and cabins and the old mission house. Now, the mission cabin is still there, but the trees have taken over the whole clearing, it doesn't look the same at all.

"I noticed something else at Little Salmon; there used to be quite a graveyard there. Now the graves, with houses and fences, are very hard to find, with twenty- and thirty-foot trees

173

growing through and right around them. I'd like to go back and see the whole river again. Maybe next year. They say that the river has taken a lot of buildings, and some of the grave-yards, away at Stewart Island. It was cutting the bank away quite badly, even twenty and thirty years ago. They had to keep moving the buildings back, and back again. I remember a two-story roadhouse that used to be there. We tied up there one time, and you could step from the boat, right over the railing and into the front door of the building. The river had simply washed the bank away, and that was it. They moved the old roadhouse over to the slough, behind the island, but all of the buildings were getting close to the bank then."

A lot of the historic sites and artifacts have just been washed away into the river. And the people have gone, too.

It was a sad thing, when the riverboats were taken off the run. But you can't stop growth and progress. And when the SS *Casca* and the *Whitehorse* burned at the shipyards below White-horse, I don't think there was a dry eye in the whole town.

As Len Usher said, "You think something like that is going to be there forever, and it's just like losing a part of your past when it goes."

Charlie Rendell's Account of the Indian Rafts

Charlie Rendell was born in Dawson City in 1913. He paints a vivid picture of the days when the river was a thriving com-merce route, not only for the White Pass riverboats, but for the huge rafts of firewood that were absolutely essential for Dawson City's very existence.

"These big booms, or rafts made from logs lashed together, were constructed by the Indians, from trees cut as far as 200 miles above Dawson. Many of the booms would have 100 cords of wood, and some even held as much as 200 cords—immense rafts. At each end of the raft they would have a huge oar, called a sweep. In the center of the raft there was a tower built up out of wood, as much as twenty feet high, for a lookout. An Indian pilot sat up on this tower. The rest of the crew would have a tent, and they'd do their own cooking. Once they left the wood camp, they never touched shore again, until they reached Dawson.

"The rafting was done in June, when there was daylight all night. They started off downriver, and never touched bottom the whole trip. The pilot would look ahead and see which direction the cord wood was taking, and as much as five miles before they came to a bend he'd start the big sweeps going, and they'd sweep from one side of the river to the other. They'd keep going in this fashion, until they got to Dawson.

"The biggest chore was when they reached the mouth of the Klondike River. They had to get it into the beach at Dawson, where there was quite a strong eddy. So by the time they got to the Klondike they'd be sweeping the raft for all its worth, towards the shore, until they entered this slack water and the eddy. And then it was a simple matter of sweeping it the rest of the way to shore.

"Some men in town would do nothing else in the summer but go out with power boats, and help these big rafts to land. Because if they missed, and went down below Dawson, it was a real inconvenience, to say the least. There was no chance in the world of bringing that wood back upstream. They would have to keep going on down river, to Forty Mile, or Eagle; any place they thought they could get rid of it. Then the crew would have to hitch a ride back home because bringing those rafts back up again was a total impossibility.

"It was bad enough for a steamboat to be going upstream, coming around a bend, and meeting 200 cords of wood coming at it; but if you were in a small motorboat it was certainly no joke! But the steamboats would crowd over to the side of the river as far as possible, and let them go by safely. The raftsmen always had the right-of-way, because they were almost uncontrollable; whereas the boats could be controlled. I don't remember ever hearing of an accident happening due to the rafting on the river.

"I've seen as many as 10,000 cords of wood piled on the beach at Dawson, in the fall of the year. Of course, the country there is all permafrost, and that was at the time when they had to do all the thawing of the frozen ground with steam. (In later years they used cold-water thawing.) Every outfit used steam boilers, not to mention the consumption of fuel in the town itself. The 10,000 cords on the exposed sandbar in front of Dawson was only a partial amount of the wood that was needed during the winter. So the wood business was a big industry.

"There was one steamboat, the *Lightning* I believe it was called, that was used exclusively for the hauling of rafts, at one time. She'd go upriver with a crew, pick up wood which they formed into a raft of 200 cords or more, and bring them down to Dawson that way."

The White Pass docks at Dawson were very sturdy and built to accomodate all the heavy machinery that was shipped into the Klondike and used to build the huge gold dredges in the early days. A longshore crew handled the steam derrick that unloaded fifteen to twenty tons per lift. The smaller freight was unloaded entirely by hand on small hand trucks. They had a small mechanical assist which hooked to the axle of the hand truck. It was all brought up and loaded into a vast warehouse on the docks.

Most freight going out of Dawson consisted of the gold shipments, which were heavy, but never used up much space. So there was always room for the thousands of sacks of silver ore from Mayo. The barges that the steamboats pushed ahead of them, took on five or six thousand tons of this ore to a load. It would be picked up on the banks at Stewart City and taken to Whitehorse for shipment outside.

Thirty miles upstream from the mouth of the Stewart River, at Maisie Mae Creek, there was a place called the Maisie Mae Ranch, which had originated back in 1897. At one time they grew as much as two or three hundred tons of hay there, which the White Pass bought for feed for the many horses used along the stage line. The ranch was later owned by Rudolph Burian and his family.

Everybody along the river had small boats, but only those who were fairly affluent could afford the larger power boats. For the smaller ones, it was always possible to go downstream; in fact one could go downstream in a handmade raft, if so desired. It was getting back upstream that presented some difficulty. People could always load a rowboat onto a stern-wheeler, and have it brought back that way, for that reason most of the local travel was done by rowboat.

"It was a friendly community in those days, the Yukon River," Charlie mused, "I really miss those times."

15

The Whitehorse Shipyards

Twenty years in the Yukon, struggling along its creeks;
Roaming its giant valleys, scaling its god-like peaks;
Bathed in its fiery sunsets, fighting its fiendish cold—
Twenty years in the Yukon...twenty years—and I'm old.

Robert Service

When I was a child, growing up in Whitehorse, one of my favorite things to do in the fall, was to go down to the shipyards and watch the big paddlewheelers being hauled out of the water, and up on the ways. And in the spring, it was even more exciting to see them come sliding back down into the river again. These boats, and the shipyards where they were maintained, were the main source of commerce in the town, and all activities during the summer months, both social and economic, revolved around them. In the winter, when the crews and workers went back outside, the little town shrunk again to its 300 permanent residents. We used to say the town went into hibernation until spring.

Walter Jensen worked for the White Pass as a shipwright in the shipyards from 1929-55, he was born in Denmark in 1894. Mr. Jensen was in charge of storing the boats for the winter and returning them again to the river when the ice went out.

Each fall, the ways had to be covered with heavy grease, or tallow. Ways were made from massive timbers laid out a few feet apart, starting up on the bank and slanting down to the river's edge. Fish oil was then put over the tallow, to make it very slippery. (All the husky dogs in town would be watching from a distance, waiting until things quieted down, so they could sneak over and lick those ways clean.)

The next job was to wrap four heavy straps, each one reinforced with four strong wires, around the steamboat. The straps were pulled right around under the boat and up the other side. A long heaving line was tied to each one of the straps, and connected to four corresponding winches, which were up on the river bank. In this manner the ships could be hauled out of the river and up to the top of the ways.

Once in place, they would be jacked into a level position, and a cradle would be built all around the ship. Then the jacks were removed.

Walter stood at the bottom of the ways flashing hand signals to the fellows who manned the winches in order to synchronize all four winches and bring the boat up smoothly and evenly. The winch hooked to the heavy stern, where the paddlewheel was located, was the important one. It would be tightened first, to ensure it would be a little higher than the rest. Then they would tighten the second one, then the third and the fourth, a little at a time, in sequence. "Now, when it's all set," Walter said, "I give them the high sign, 'All together!' Then they pull the levers, and the winches go all together."

There were unexpected accidents, sometimes, when the boats were being hauled up. If something went wrong with a winch, and the boat started sliding back towards the river, Walter would tell the men to let it go loose. If they tried to stop the free slide by tightening the other winches, it could break the ship in two, so he signalled them to let it go. "Some of the men would jump and scream, and holler if they thought I was giving the wrong signal, but I paid no attention at all. They didn't understand. You'd have to let that ship slide back into the river and start all over again—balanced right. But it was funny to hear those inexperienced guys screaming like crazy."

The last time the *Tutshi* was hauled out in Carcross, Walter was there, working on the job. It was in November, and very cold that day. "We pulled the boat out of the water, and the ways were just like a skating rink," Walter said. "When it was out, the fellow I was working with got the idea to drop his wires. I was looking after the ones in the stern, but I hadn't got the cleat (a piece of wood or metal used to prevent slipping) on them yet. Well, that fellow dropped his before I was ready, and the darn thing went back in the water again. Holy Moses, you never saw such a mess in all your life, as those wires! Those are great big huge wheels, you know, with all that wire on them. They were spinning so you couldn't see them for dust. My partner wanted to try and curb them, but I said, no just get out of here. Because if that wheel decided to come at us, it could kill you dead, you know. Well, no sooner had we got out of the way, when there went the wheel! It took off clean through the air, and it was spinning so fast it got down to the head lock, it smashed all to pieces. That three-quarter-inch wire was all tied in knots."

When it came time to launch the ships in the spring, it was a matter of reversing, to a certain point, the procedure that had been followed in the fall. The ship was secured with a cable and jacks, while the cribs were taken off the bottom side of the boat. Then the top crib was removed and the boat was eased onto the ways again. The big lasso, the only thing holding it at that point, was cut, and the ship began its slide down to the water, picking up speed as it went along. It hit the water with a big splash, sending a spray up into the air. The man who rode down on it, had to snub up the rope to keep the boat from getting too far away from shore.

Lorne Coleman remembered the time he first had the job of riding the paddlewheeler down the ways. "I was lucky to get away with not losing an arm," said Lorne. "I didn't throw the hitch around fast enough. It's quite tricky, the first time. You have to throw the rope around the bollard, so it will slip and come to a halt gradually, otherwise you would snap the line. I fumbled it a bit that time, but luckily I came to no harm."

The year of 1936 was the busiest year that Walter Jensen could remember at the shipyards. "They lost two ships, that year, the *Klondike* and the *Casca*, and we had to build new ones to replace them. The *Klondike* was built from scratch right in Whitehorse. The *Casca* was framed in Vancouver, at the old coal shed under Granville St. bridge, and shipped up to Whitehorse for completion."

There were ten shipwrights working for White Pass that year. "It was quite simple work, compared with building ships in Vancouver. You set up the framework, and then go on to the planking, then the inside work, just taking one step at a time. Those sternwheelers are just flat bottomed, and they have straight sides. The housework on them had to be made as light as possible, and they were just like kindling. If a boat sank in the river up to its top deck, the ice going out next spring would clean the wheelhouse off just like nothing. It only took one season to build those two boats."

One time, the shipwrights had the job of 'stretching' the SS *Nasutlin*. They cut it in half and put thirty extra feet in the middle part; quite a feat of accomplishment. Even today, in British Columbia, stretching a ship is considered to be a fairly modern procedure.

The boiler work and steampipe construction was all done by the engineers and the firemen, who worked on the boats themselves. Lorne Coleman was one of these men. He worked as a tinsmith in the shipyards, in the early spring, while the crews waited for the ice to melt in the river. Lorne made all the heaters for the boats, steam tables, coffee urns, bread pans, roasting pans, garbage cans, and many other items that would be needed when the boats started running. His boss was a man by the name of Ed MacDonald. "Most of the shipwrights were from Scotland," Lorne said, "and when someone in the shop yelled, 'Hey, Mac!' ten different voices would answer, 'Aye, Jock?'" When the boats started running, Lorne worked as fireman for the rest of the season.

The main job in maintaining the ships, Walter Jensen said, was replacing the planks that had worn out, or been damaged by the rocks. The ones that took most of the beating, were called the 'knuckle' planks. They were the ones on the right and left corners, on the front of the ship. They would hit first, if the boat touched the bank or came up against anything solid. These planks were held on with bolts, so they could be taken off easily, and replaced.

"Coming upstream, you could have walked alongside those boats, and kept right up with them," Walter said, "But going back down sometimes, they'd be going too fast to make some of the sharp turns in the river, so they'd have to back up and try again—just inching their way around. So they could skin themselves up a bit once in a while."

It was never worth trying to salvage a wrecked riverboat. They were built to be written off, because they had to be so light.

In a normal year, once the boats were repaired, painted and launched, the work was over for several of the men, so the White Pass put them to work at other jobs, such as repairing bridges on the railway, or whatever else needed doing. Sometimes they went to work in Skagway for a while. They were promised a season's work when they signed on, so the company made sure they were occupied with something.

A general yard crew was maintained all summer, using mostly local help when they could get it, and in the winter there was a caretaker at the shipyards.

Henry Breadon's Account of Steamboat Launchings

According to Henry, on the large steamboats they used as many as six straps, with six cables in each, to wrap around the boats for pulling them up on the greased ways. They used large timbers between the boats and the straps, to keep the straps from biting into the sides of the ships. Steam winches were ideal for the job, because the pressure on all six of them was identical, not like the original method using individual combustion engines. They could pull up the boat sideways easily, with the stern and bow right in line.

Then the boat was jacked up, and the shipyard foreman inspected the bottom planks. He would mark the ones that were rotting or scarred with chalk, and these boards would later be knocked out. A crib would be constructed around the boat to hold it level over the winter months. The actual repair work was done the following May, when the crews returned from outside for the summer.

After they were all 'shipshape' again, they would have to be jacked back down, until they were sitting on the ways for launching. Originally, Henry said, the company used screw jacks, and the boat would sit on sixteen to eighteen jacks along each side. When the shipyard foreman blew his whistle, every man, at the same time, would make a quarter turn in his jack. Then they would put the bar into the next hole, and make another quarter turn when the whistle blew again. This is how the boat was brought down evenly. It was time consuming. It took up to three hours before it was ready for launching.

The ways were greased with mutton tallow the night before a launching, so the tallow would acquire the same temperature as the surroundings, and harden up. The brush they used for this job was made by cutting a length of inch and a half rope, and fraying it out at one end. Then in the morning, the men would take heated fish oil, and slather it all over the tallow, with a wide paddle.

For launching, they used 'butterboards,' which fit right in between the hull and the ways, and the stern and the ways. These boards helped keep the boat level, and acted as a great assist when the boat was ready to slide down. The very last step was to slash the lashings which, at that point, were the only things holding the ship.

"Sometimes," Henry said, "the boat didn't wait for the lashings to be cut. When it was lowered to the ways, it just took right off on those slippery things—it tore those lashings out and away she went. This happened in 1948 with the *Keno*. They had finished dropping the lower side, but the upper side was still up on the jacks, and the blocking was kicked loose. I was on the stem jack, and I could feel when the boat first started to move. The bar was facing out towards the river, and it started to go down in my hand. The boat hadn't broken the lashings, as of yet, but I knew enough to get clear myself. I swung around on the jack, so it (the jack) wouldn't fall on me.

"My partner almost got into a bind that time, because when the ship started to go, he started to run toward the river, which is the way it was going. Well, down near the river there would be no more than six inches of space between the hull of the vessel and the shore ice, when it got there. We hollered at him, 'Drop! Drop!' and fortunately he did, while the ship was still high enough to pass over him. It was sure moving that morning. The grease temperature must have been just right, because as a rule, you have to give them a little nudge to get them started, and they would pick up speed and momentum as they went on down to the river. There would always be two fellows on the ship riding her down, and they'd have four-inch Manila rope lines on her, which they'd let out gradually as she went along. When they hit the water she would go out about 20 or 30 feet, and then they'd snub the lines and bring her back in.

"It wasn't uncommon for other people to go on the upper decks, and ride the thing down either. It was pretty exhilarating when you hit the water from up there."

Bells, Gongs and Telegraphs

Before the telegraph system came into use on the paddle-wheelers, a system of signals was standard on all the boats. It was a unique system, all done with bells and gongs. Using a combination of these, the skipper could signal the engine room for whatever speed he wanted, whether it be ahead or astern.

Starting at the dock, for instance; when the ship was ready to move out, the skipper would ring three bells. It could be heard all over the vessel, and if the engineer was ready, he would ring three bells back. Full ahead was one bell. Full astern was two bells. A combination of a bell, and a jingle, meant half ahead; and a bell and two jingles, slow ahead. By these signals the engineer knew how much power to put on. There were many combinations of bells and jingles, and after awhile they would become second nature to the crew. When the ship was pushing a barge especially, the signals were crucial. When the engineer got the signal for more steam, it was noticeable immediately in the amount of steam that the yellow stacks would puff out.

When the telegraph system came into being, it was far

184

more efficient, but some of the romance of the riverboats was taken away.

The boats also used 'voice tubes.' These were two metal tubes about an inch in diameter, one between the wheelhouse and the engine room, and the other went from the engine room to the foredeck. There was a little whistle built into each end. A person could blow into this, and someone at the other end would answer by whistling on the other end, and then he would put his ear to it and listen to what the skipper or captain had to say.

The Last Trip of the SS *Keno*

On August 25, 1960, the *Keno* was taken downriver to Dawson City for the last time. It was her retirement voyage, and she was to be placed on the banks of the river there, as a historical monument representing the fascinating era of the paddle-wheelers on the Yukon River. Henry Breaden was on that trip, and the following paragraphs contain his memories of the occasion.

Emil Forrest was the one overseeing the restoration of the boat, caulking the hull, and getting it seaworthy, but tragically he suffered a heart attack before the boat left Whitehorse and missed the voyage he had been looking forward to so much.

The main problem encountered in getting the ship ready was vandalism—over the years, anything that was made of copper or brass had gone missing. All the copper wires had been stripped off the generators, and many of the brass valves and lubricators in the engine room were gone, too.

"The telegraph was still there," Henry said, "fortunately for us." (They went downstream without the generator.) "The trip from Whitehorse to Upper Laberge was fairly uneventful. We had lost a couple of hours, waiting for a CBC filming crew that was on its way. So it was getting dark when we got to Upper Laberge. I was out in front with a high-powered flashlight, looking for any markers that might be left. Pilot Frank Slim was at the wheel and I was trying to find that first marker. We found it just in time to save going aground on a submerged sandbar. We laid over that night at Upper Laberge.

"There was an engineer from National Parks aboard, a fellow whose last name was Post, and a skipper from Radium. The fireman was Len Bath, and all the deckhands were complete greenhorns. I acted as mate on the trip down, as that had been my job, years before."

The wood required for the trip downriver was carried right on the boat, this time.

"There was one event just after we entered the 30 Mile River, at U.S. Bend; we were coming around the curve, and the hydraulic tiller, which they had rigged up specially for this trip, jammed. Normally, in the old days, they would just give the wheel a little spin and that would be all it needed, but we didn't have the wheel to do this now. Frank was wrestling with the tiller, and Holy Moses! I could see they weren't going to make it without going ashore. I rang 'Full Astern,' but the chief at this time wasn't used to this river navigation. I was just running up and down thinking, 'Holy Smoke, pick it up chief, pick it up!' Well, finally he did, but I'll tell you, we weren't that far from going on the beach.

"At one point the camera crew found that there was too much light getting in for filming the interior of the cabin, so they started covering up the windows. I had to go around yelling at them to stop. After all, I told them, we have to see where we're going. From there on, everything was fine until we got to Carmacks. We tied up at the old coal mine and went down to look at the bridge, to make sure we had enough clearance to get the boat under. There were no bridges across rivers when the boats were still running, so we had to take the wheelhouse off, and put it on the boat deck to get enough clearance, and we took the stack down (it had been fixed up with a special hinge for this trip). From then on, the steering was pretty awkward. It's a lot harder to see where you're going, from the observation room, and you don't have the advantage of that height up in the wheelhouse. You could see what was going on right in front of the boat, and either side, but you couldn't see what was going on behind. So it took two fellows, the pilot and another one out the side, telling him what was going on. We had about a foot and a half clearance under that bridge. We backed her through, then tied the boat up, and raised the stack and wheelhouse again. We crossed Five Fingers and Rink Rapids, without any trouble, but when we came to Slackwater Crossing, above Minto, the channel had filled in.

"I was sitting there, eating a can of beans, and when I saw Frank jump out of his chair I knew something was amiss, so I threw my beans aside and ran out on the bow, and Holy Smoke! there was no water there at all. We started going full astern, but before we got it stopped we ran aground. That was about six o'clock at night, and it took us until seven-thirty before we got it into deep water again. CBC was there filming the whole process. We had to run lines ashore, of course. I used a scheme that we employed many years earlier, and that was wrapping the lines around big clumps of Yukon willow, about six clumps in a line. We wrapped the cable around each one of the these, and shackled into the last one. Then we came back through, and tightened the line up. It was amazing what they would hold. The first clump would pull a little bit; the second a bit less, and the third still less, and finally you had equal strain on them all, and they pulled that boat right off the sandbar.

"We had Terry Delaney with a scuba diving suit down over the side, and he put the blocks in our stern ring. It was a lot different from the old days when you had to go down there with all your clothes on. It was just a matter of...'hop in fellas!' then. We earned our wages in those days. Especially when a barge went ashore with a load of maybe 200 tons on board. That was the tough one!

"There used to be a place between Stewart River and Dawson, that was called Dog Island. Well, when we arrived at that place...it had entirely disappeared. Gone, just like that! I couldn't believe my eyes.

"Yes, there were a few changes alright. The steady churning of the boat traffic in the old days had kept the channels from silting up. Now, after all these years, the channels had filled up with silt and gravel, and gradually just levelled out, and the river was much shallower now than it used to be. The river banks had cut way back in places, too. And, of course, there was no traffic on the river.

"We used to see G. I. Cameron patrolling up and down, all the time. And old Finley Beaton was out there a lot, too. The fish camps were all gone, and of course the woodcutters. No white flags, no people on the banks to see the *Keno* chuffing down the river for her last time.

"The first job for the crew on the *Keno*, was negotiating with the city of Dawson, and the parks board as to where the boat would be positioned. The remnants of the old White Pass dock, and the fire hall were still there from the earlier fire that had gutted them, and it was decided that this area would be the best place for the *Keno*. The next two days were spent levelling off a spot for the ways to be put in, with a couple of big Caterpillars. All the slings, steel snatch blocks and cable for pulling had been brought down on the ship, plus the mutton tallow for greasing the ways.

"Many of the Indian fellows in Dawson had worked with me over the years," said Henry, "and by talking to them I found out that down in the old shipyards, below the city, there was about half a drum of fish oil, left over from the riverboat days. This was just what I needed to put that extra slick on the ways. So on the weekend I took one of the Cats across the river on the ferry, and went down to the shipyards with this fellow, and we found the oil and a lot of old things that had been left over. Some extra snatch blocks were there, and we found everything we needed for pulling the *Keno* up."

When Henry was doing the excavation work with the Cat, he came across cases and cases of horse shoes that must have been there since the days the White Pass was using horses for the overland mail stage. It was an old blacksmith's shop. "Well, before I knew it," said Henry, "I had horseshoes hanging off the blade and over the tracks, and horseshoes all over the ground. I was excavating right into the river, there, just off First Avenue, looking for anchors. I was only able to go down about three feet in the permafrost, and just in those three feet, I ran across a whole lot of the old Dawson history.

"After the carpenters had constructed the ways, the SS

Keno was hauled up to its final resting place, where it remains today as a National Historic Site and a nostalgic reminder of the riverboat days.

"When we chuffed into Dawson the whole town was out to greet us. And I'll bet there were some old-timers hiding a few tears, too."

MORE GREAT HANCOCK HOUSE TITLES

Northern Biographies

Alaska Calls
Virginia Neely
ISBN 0-88839-970-7

Bootlegger's Lady
Sager & Frye
ISBN 0-88839-976-6

Bush Flying
Robert S. Grant
ISBN 0-88839-350-4

Crazy Cooks & Gold Miners
Joyce Yardley
ISBN 0-88839-294-X

Descent into Madness
Vernon Frolick
ISBN 0-88839-300-8

Fogswamp: Life with Swans
Turner & McVeigh
ISBN 0-88839-104-8

Gang Ranch: Real Story
Judy Alsager
ISBN 0-88839-275-3

Journal of a Country Lawyer
E. C. Burton
ISBN 0-88839-364-4

Lady Rancher
Gertrude Roger
ISBN 0-88839-099-8

My Heart Soars
Chief Dan George
ISBN 0-88839-231-1

My Spirit Soars
Chief Dan George
ISBN 0-88839-233-8

Nahanni
Dick Turner
ISBN 0-88839-028-9

Novice in the North
Bill Robinson
ISBN 0-88839-977-4

Ralph Edwards of Lonesome Lake
Ed Gould
ISBN 0-88839-100-5

Ruffles on my Longjohns
Isabel Edwards
ISBN 0-88839-102-1

Where Mountains Touch Heaven
Ena Kingsnorth Powell
ISBN 0-88839-365-2

Wings of the North
Dick Turner
ISBN 0-88839-060-2

Yukon Lady
Hugh McLean
ISBN 0-88839-186-2

Yukoners
Harry Gordon-Cooper
ISBN 0-88839-232-X

History

Barkerville
Lorraine Harris
ISBN 0-88839-152-8

B.C.'s Own Railroad
Lorraine Harris
ISBN 0-88839-125-0

MORE GREAT HANCOCK HOUSE TITLES

Buckskin, Blades and Biscuits
Allen Kent Johnston
ISBN 0-88839-363-6

Cariboo Gold Rush Story
Donald Waite
ISBN 0-88839-202-8

The Craigmont Story
Murphy Shewchuk
ISBN 0-88839-980-4

Curse of Gold
Elizabeth Hawkins
ISBN 0-88839-281-8

Early History of Port Moody
Dorothea M. Norton
ISBN 0-88839-197-8

End of Custer
Dale T. Schoenberger
ISBN 0-88839-288-5

Fishing in B.C.
Forester & Forester
ISBN 0-919654-43-6

Fraser Canyon Highway
Lorraine Harris
ISBN 0-88839-182-X

Fraser Canyon Story
Donald E. Waite
ISBN 0-88839-204-4

Fraser Valley Story
Donald E. Waite
ISBN 0-88839-203-6

Gold Creeks & Ghost Towns
N. L. (Bill) Barlee
ISBN 0-88839-988-X

Gold! Gold!
Joseph Petralia
ISBN 0-88839-118-8

Living with Logs
Donovan Clemson
ISBN 0-919654-44-4

Lost Mines & Historic Treasures
N. L. (Bill) Barlee
ISBN 0-88839-992-8

The Mackenzie Yesterday
Alfred P. Aquilina
ISBN 0-88839-083-1

Pioneering Aviation of the West
Lloyd M. Bungey
ISBN 0-88839-271-0

Power Quest
Carol Batdorf
ISBN 0-88839-240-0

Spirit Quest
Carol Batdorf
ISBN 0-88839-210-9

Totem Poles of the NW
D. Allen
ISBN 0-919654-83-5

Vancouver Recalled
Derek Pethick
ISBN 0-919654-09-6

When Buffalo Ran
George Bird Grinnell
ISBN 0-88839-258-3

Yukon Gold
Jim and Susan Preyde
ISBN 0-88839-362-8

Other Hancock House Titles

Robert Service
51/2 X 81/2, 64 pp. SC
ISBN 0-88839-223-0

Robert Service
51/2 X 81/2, 64 pp. SC
ISBN 0-88839-224-9

Jack London
51/2 X 81/2, 104 pp. SC
ISBN 0-88839-259-1

Chief Dan George and
Helmut Hirnschall
51/2 X 81/2, 96 pp. SC
ISBN 0-88839-231-1

Chief Dan George and
Helmut Hirnschall
51/2 X 81/2, 96 pp. SC
ISBN 0-88839-233-8

Mike Puhallo, Brian Brannon,
and Wendy Liddle
51/2 X 81/2, 64 pp. SC
ISBN 0-88839-368-7

Robert F. Harrington
51/2 X 81/2, 96 pp. SC
ISBN 0-88839-367-9

pj johnson
51/2 X 81/2, 64 pp. SC
ISBN 0-88839-366-0

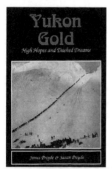

James and Susan Preyde
51/2 X 81/2, 96 pp. SC
ISBN 0-88839-362-8

Available from Hancock House Publishers   19313 Zero Ave., Surrey, B.C. V4P 1M7
1-800-938-1114   Credit cards accepted.   1431 Harrison Ave., Blaine, WA 98230